"HYPNOTIC STORYTELLING . . . earthy, mystical, bloody and unashamedly emotional."

—*Los Angeles Times*

"THIS BOOK THRIVES ON THE EXUBERANCE OF ITS PROSE, the vitality of the story, the power of its images, and the author's compassion for the human condition."

—*Albuquerque Journal*

"A WONDERFUL BOOK FROM ONE OF MY FAVORITE WRITERS. Beautiful, evocative and moving."

—Oscar Hijuelos, author of
The Mambo Kings Play Songs of Love

RAIN OF GOLD

"A BIG BOOK . . . A STORY THAT DESERVES TO BE TOLD . . . EXTREMELY MOVING . . . A COMPELLING NARRATIVE."

—*The Washington Post Book World*

"A TRIUMPH . . . *RAIN OF GOLD* IS ONE OF THE BEST— and the most American—books of this or any other year."

—*USA Today*

"A GRAND AND VIVID HISTORY . . . The characters are keenly drawn . . . often I felt like a family member watching from a corner stool."

—*The New York Times*

WALKING STARS
Stories of Magic and Power

VICTOR VILLASEÑOR

Delta
Trade Paperbacks

A Delta Book
Published by
Dell Publishing
a division of
Bantam Doubleday Dell Publishing Group, Inc.
1540 Broadway
New York, New York 10036

This book is made possible through a grant from the National Endowment for the Arts (a federal agency), the Lila Wallace-Reader's Digest Fund, and the Andrew W. Mellon Foundation.

ISBN: 0-385-31654-2

Reprinted by arrangement with Piñata Books

Manufactured in the United States of America
Published simultaneously in Canada

June 1998

10 9 8

BVG

Table of Contents

WALKING STARS
Stories of Magic and Power

Preface

I have two boys in high school, and ever since they were little, I've been telling them that there's a way to live life, *la vida*, with power and magic, a way of triumphing over all odds and living life like a superhuman being, just like Superwoman and Superman. And this isn't "bull," but the "truth" of all living, if only we open up our eyes to see life, *la vida*, in all its true wonder and greatness.

And so I tell my boys stories, true stories about my life and their grandparents' and their great-grandparents' lives, stories that give them wings of understanding and feet of power rooted in Mother Earth, so that they can then live their lives not alone, but with the breath of their ancestry breathing down their necks. And I tell them that these stories will give them strength and a sense of well-being, even in their darkest hours of living in this scary "modern" world, where people are afraid of getting old, afraid of being left alone, or simply afraid to reach out and touch their fellow human beings.

You see, I tell my boys and their cousins and friends, life is full of magic, real magic, and not the magic of tricks and games and pulling rabbits out of black hats, but the real magic that gives us power and strength to endure and triumph in everyday life, *la vida*.

And you can turn up your noses at me if you want and say that that's for the old people and the old ways and not for "now" in modern times, but I'll tell you straight to your face, "Bull! Bull! Bull!" For this is the magic of the ages, and it's good for all time! For 5,000 × 5,000 years into the future or into the past! If you have the eyes to see and the ears to hear, you will know that to live life without the magic of your God-given soul is to live life like a fish out of water, like an eagle without sky, an antelope without an open meadow or a heart without love. You see, the soul is to magic just like the eagle is to the sky and the fish is to water and the antelope is to the big, open meadow—our soul is fearless and full of joy and makes living a great, glorious, magical adventure open to all!

So, my boys ask me where I get all this special knowledge. I tell them that it all started when I was born in the *barrio* of Carlsbad, California, and everyone spoke Spanish, and my mother would put me to bed at night and call me her little angel boy, *su angelito*, and tell me that when I went to sleep, I'd go up to heaven and rest with *Papito Dios*, Little Daddy God, and then I'd return in the morning all rested and good.

And back then, when I was little and I hadn't started school yet, I thought God was a chubby, little, daddy-like figure who was friendly and happy and ate beans and tortillas and shot down a tequila now and then, and that He liked to laugh a lot and have a good time. I never had the idea that God was tall and strong and authoritative and would send you to hell if you misbehaved, until I started school.

You see, for me school was a very scary experience. I hardly spoke any English, and on my first day, the teacher yelled at us, the Mexican kids, "No Spanish!" and punished us if she caught us speaking one word, and hit us on the head if we continued. And in no time at all, the magic that I'd known in my pre-school life was ripped away from me. If I mentioned that the sun was the Right Eye of God, as I'd been told at home, I was ridiculed. If I said anything about Mexico or anything about my Native Indian culture, I was laughed at. And looking back as an adult, I can now see that the teacher probably wasn't that "bad" and was only trying to invite us into the mainstream of the United States, so we could prosper and make life easier for ourselves. But back then as a child, that was not how it felt. No, it felt more as if a war had been declared on us, as if the wars between Spain and England for world dominance were still going on right there in our classroom, and she set out to prove to us that everything English was superior and everything Spanish and Indian was inferior and evil and wrong.

And I don't want you to think that looking back, now as an adult, that I'm blaming those teachers who hit us and embarrassed us and tried so hard to make us feel ashamed of our parents and our Native American and Spanish culture. No, those teachers are what caused me to erupt with such rage and hate, such fire against injustice within my God-given soul, that nothing could've stopped me. And I decided to become a writer. I had such a conviction, such a need, that I was able to write for ten years and get 265 rejections and never give up until I got published.

So, you see, I'd like you to truly understand that I'm not that smart or great, and I didn't become a writer because I did well in school and got A's. No, I became a writer because I had so much confusion and anguish inside of me that I wished to kill with a vengeance from hell itself.

Always be careful of whom you put down or pick on,

because I can guarantee you that they will grow strong and come back to haunt you with the power of ten thousand angels, and fly right past you, reaching for the stars. This is the power of the Jews—my wife and kids are Jewish, and so now I am, too, through osmosis. They've been beaten and persecuted all over the world, and so that's why they've become strong and capable. This is the power of the blacks here in our country; they were beaten and persecuted so much that they've risen up as some of our finest minds and artists and athletes. This is the power of any people who are put down: Yellow, Red, Black, White or Brown. They will rise up a thousand times more powerful, just like weeds breaking through asphalt. Nothing can stop the human spirit, especially when it's aware of its own power.

These, then, I tell my boys, aren't nice, little stories of magic and fantasy, but stories of gut-awful pain and heart-break, confusion and self-hate and doubt, and then, finally, that great, "real" magic power of life that's sitting there, within each of us, waiting to erupt and help us overcome against all odds.

These, then, are stories for all people, men and women, boys and girls, who've ever suffered or been wronged, who've ever felt lonely or misunderstood, or have ever gotten so beaten down by society that life seemed all scary and upside down. These are true stories about real life and real people, not made-up, phony, movie heroes with big muscles who always know all the answers, but stories of people like you and me: ordinary people who don't quite know where they're going or how to get there, but, always seem to find the way to survive and flourish.

Remember, like my mother told me each night when

she put me to bed back in the barrio, we're all angels—not humans, but angels, full-time spiritual beings feeling a little human while we live in this short, tiny dream called life, *la vida.*

And, also, please understand that if it hadn't been for that love that my mother gave me each night in Spanish as she put me down to sleep, I'm sure that I wouldn't have had the power, the magic, to endure all the bullying and terrible things that happened to me later in life. It was as if I had love on one side, keeping me going, and hate on the other side, knocking me down. But somehow, between these two very powerful emotions, I managed to grow like a weed that comes up through the cement, breaking stone and concrete, getting its power from Mother Earth as it reaches for Father Sky. This is what the human spirit is: an indestructible force, bursting forth against all odds, rooted in love, as it reaches for God's golden sunlight.

Thank you. I hope you enjoy these stories as much as my family and I have.

Reach for the stars. It's cheaper, in the long run. *¡Adelante, amigos y amigas!*

—Victor E. Villaseñor
Rancho Villaseñor
Oceanside, California 92054

Part One:
My Birth to Power and Magic

The Smartest Human I Ever Met: My Brother's Dog Shep

I was eight years old the night my brother's dog went crazy-*loco* and started racing around the house, howling to the heavens. It was late at night, I was sound asleep, and my parents were down in San Diego at Scripps Hospital seeing my brother, who'd been sick for nearly a year. Joseph was sixteen years old, and he'd been hit in a football game and just bruised a little bit internally, but our local doctor—a drunk—hadn't attended to him correctly, and his liver was ruined and he developed leukemia.

I could hear his dog Shep racing around the house, howling like crazy. Quickly, I got up to go see what was the matter. Shep was a very smart dog and didn't bark for just any reason. I pulled on my boots and got my BB gun and went out the front door. There was a half-moon and the stars were out by the thousands. We lived on a ranch in north San Diego County not far from the sea, and often animals came down the canyon behind our home on their way to the ocean. I looked around but saw nothing. As far as I could see, the dog was just chasing around after himself, acting crazy. I called him.

"Shep!" I shouted to him. "It's all right. Just come in. Nothing's the matter."

I wanted him to come to me so I could pet him and calm him down, but he wouldn't come near me. No, he just kept racing around and howling like he was *loco*. And Shep was a smart, level-headed dog, too. He was half coyote and half Shepherd and I'd been hunting and going horseback riding with him for as long as I could remember. He'd always listened to me before, so I couldn't figure out what was going on. He was acting really strange. He just kept racing around and around the house, howling something fierce.

My little sister Linda woke up and came outside to see what was the matter, too. Then, the Mexican-Indian woman, Rosa, who was taking care of us while my parents were gone, came outside to check on us.

"Is everything all right?" asked Rosa in Spanish. We all spoke Spanish on the ranch. English wasn't a language any of us spoke unless we went out the gates of the property.

"Yes," I said in Spanish, "it's just that our dog has gone crazy. He's barking at nothing and won't come to me."

"He's not barking at nothing," Rosa said to me. "He's barking because your brother is dying."

I was stunned. I didn't know what to think. "But my brother isn't dying," I said. "He's getting well. That's why my parents have him in the hospital."

Rosa's husband, Emilio, suddenly came out of the dark, and I now saw that several other of the farmhands were all sitting quietly under the huge pepper tree.

"Rosa is right," he said gently. "Your brother is dying.

That's why his dog is going crazy; he loves your brother very much."

"Yes, he loves my brother, but, well," I stopped. I didn't know what to say. My parents had told my sister and me that they had the best doctors money could buy attending to my brother, and that he was getting well. I glanced from Emilio to Rosa and then back again. "But how can this dog know that my brother is dying? My brother is more than thirty miles away! You're wrong! You're wrong! You just don't know what you're talking about!"

"All right," said Emilio, putting his arm about his wife's shoulders, "have it your way. But understand, the soul knows no distance, and love speaks through the heart. And that dog is telling us of his heart breaking for your brother."

"No!" I yelled. "My brother isn't dying! Shep has got to stop howling!"

But no matter how much I yelled at him, Shep wouldn't stop. I began to cry, too. I was scared now, and my heart was breaking, just like Shep's.

The workmen never said a thing. They just sat there under the huge pepper tree, poking at the ground with sticks and being very quiet. Rosa finally took my sister and me back inside.

All that night, my brother's dog kept howling, and then, in the early morning, he suddenly stopped, just like that. When I went outside to see what had happened, I was told that he'd taken off for the hills.

My parents came home later that day and informed my sister and me that our brother Joseph had died. They said that the doctors had done all they could with their modern medicine, but still he was gone.

I could see that mother's whole face was swollen from crying when she went into the house. My father stayed outside with my sister and me. I wanted to tell my father that we'd found out about my brother's death the night before because of his dog, but I just didn't know how to say this without sounding stupid.

Later that day, I went to tell Emilio and Rosa that they were right, that my brother had died, but they said they already knew.

"We saw his dog take off this morning for the hills to intercept his soul," said Rosa.

I'll never forget the chills that went up and down my spine on hearing those words "to intercept his soul," and I got this powerful image of my brother's dog running up to the highest hilltop he could find and leaping into the sky to join with my brother's soul as it made its way to heaven.

We never saw my brother's dog after that. And when I asked Rosa and her husband what had happened to Shep, they explained to me that he'd left his body up in the hills somewhere so he could travel to the other side of life with my brother, whom he'd loved very much. Animals, she'd explained to me, could do that at will, much easier than humans, because they hadn't learned how to talk and question yet, and love was still their basis for living life.

Shortly after that, Rosa and Emilio returned to Mexico. They left a couple of days after I told my father of the things that they'd told me about Shep and my brother. My dad got real angry and said, "Your mother and I got the finest doctor we could find for your brother, and no stupid old Indian beliefs are going to create doubt of my word!"

But, no matter how much my father raged and shouted, I still knew that I'd seen my brother's dog go crazy-*loco* with his love for my brother and then disappear the next day to never be seen again.

*　　*　　*

Author's Note

This story has always haunted me, but it wasn't until twenty-some years later, when I started interviewing my father and mother so I could write down our family's history, that I began to truly understand just how important that night had been. It had been the time in my parents' lives when they'd moved out of the *barrio*, started doing business with Anglos, and they'd put their trust in modern doctors and medicine and they'd come up empty. They'd moved away from their cultural roots and basic beliefs and were feeling completely lost and all alone in this new world of theirs.

And Shep, well, he really was the smartest human I ever met. Not only did he teach me about hunting and stalking, he also awakened me to the world of magic and dreams and gave me the basic tools that I needed so that, years later, when I went down to Mexico to La Barranca el Cobre to do research for my mother's life story, the true gems of life were able to shine for me.

You see, Rosa and her husband were right. Shep did know that my brother was dying because, simply, dogs can smell what we can't smell, hear what we can't hear, and feel what we can't feel.

But, of course, I didn't know any of this when I was a boy of eight years of age. In fact, the longer I live, the more I realize that so many of our most important lessons in life aren't known to us until decades later. So, always keep an open mind and keep going, for you never know when today's catastrophe will be tomorrow's miracle.

Midnight Duke

Midnight Duke was a large, good-looking, all-black gelding that always kept to himself and didn't bother any of the other horses. And he wasn't our fastest horse or smartest horse or even our best-trained or anything else. No, he was just a good, honest horse that had a certain way about him. And anytime a mare was going to foal, Duke would begin to get nervous and walk back and forth in his corral. Then the next day—different than cattle, horses always seemed to have their young at night—we'd always find that Duke had, somehow, gotten out his corral and he was with the mare and her newborn, standing like a sentry some sixty feet away. And pity any dog or coyote that tried to come and bother that mare and her little foal. Why, once we even found a jackrabbit that'd ventured too close, and Duke had caught the rabbit and stomped him into the ground until there was nothing left of the poor little animal but skin and thrashed pieces of flesh and bone.

And we all knew that no horse alive can catch a jackrabbit, that it's impossible. Even the fastest, quickest quarter horse couldn't do it. But there lay the remains of that jackrabbit, and Duke was still snorting something fierce when we came upon him in the morning.

The ranch hands explained to me that when Duke was castrated, he must have been left with strong male feelings. So, not being able to have children of his own, he'd decided to do the next best thing, and that was to protect foals with all his God-given power while they were being born. And protect, Duke would do. Why, he'd even kicked down gates and climbed over fences just to be by that mare's side that he knew was going to give birth. And at no other time was Duke that aggressive or unusual. So it took us all by complete surprise the day that Big Diamond was brought to our ranch and Duke became a fighting machine.

You see, at that time, I was ten or eleven and my dad had opened up a riding stable so we could rent horses out. Too many of my parents' friends were just stopping by on weekends and drinking my father's whiskey and wanting to go horseback riding. So my dad decided to make our ranch into a place of business, so he wouldn't have to keep saying no to his friends.

An old cowboy who'd been born in Arizona the century before was brought on to run the stables. His name was Si Barnett and he chewed tobacco and had false teeth and smelled stronger than a horse with a two-month sweat. He never relieved himself indoors, and he always slept in the tact room so he could smell the saddles all night long, and he always liked to tell jokes.

Then one day, Si brought in a string of horses from over by Escondido—a place east of us about twenty miles—and put them in with our horses. In this group there was one huge, black, big-bone horse called Diamond because he had a white diamond on his forehead. And immediately, even I at my young age could see that Diamond was their ring-leader, and that he was up to no good. You see, having so many horses come through our ranch, I'd come to realize that horses were just like people, and each one had his own personality and way of behaving.

And, well, Diamond just took one quick look around at the place and decided that, since this was his new home, he was going to quickly establish who was boss around there. He quickly—for no reason whatsoever—attacked two or three of our horses, biting and kicking each and showing them how tough he was. Si and my Dad and the other two men just watched, doing nothing.

"Let them settle things amongst themselves quickly," said Si, "and then it's over, and we'll have no more problems. Just like chickens or any other herd animals, there's got to be a pecking order or there will never be peace."

And so Diamond quickly attacked another horse and another horse, driving each off their hay and establishing his power. We had twenty-some head in the corral, and by now they were just moving away from Diamond or putting up a little fight for self-respect, but then running like hell.

Then, Diamond was almost done; he'd moved every horse off his or her hay or place and he was now the new boss. But then, he made the terrible mistake of attacking a mare with a new foal that was by the water trough. And Midnight Duke, who never fought anyone and had never been the boss of anything, suddenly before our very eyes turned into this monster. He came racing across the corral with such conviction of heart and soul that he bit the bigger, stronger horse by the back of the neck and knocked him to the ground. And then Midnight Duke was pawing and whirling and kicking. Diamond got to his feet and took off racing out of the corral and down the hill as if the Devil were after him. But Duke never let up; he was still on the big, black newcomer all the way down that hillside and halfway across the valley, biting and pawing and screeching something fierce.

Si and my Dad were laughing in wild hysterics.

"Jesus Christ!" said Si. "In all my seventy years of breaking and training horses from Arizona to Wyoming, I've never seen the likes of that! Why, if Diamond hadn't run, Duke would've killed him, sure as hell!"

Two weeks later, Si told us how he stayed up all night and watched Duke climb over a seven-foot fence, just like a human being going up a ladder, to get to the mare that was foaling.

"That darn gelding has got more spirit and determination than any horse I've ever seen!" said Si, eyes gleaming with excitement. "My God, what a stud he might have been, throwing colts of the best!"

And the picture of Duke climbing that fence under the full moon to go and protect a mare with her foal grew and grew inside my head until I, too, knew that Midnight Duke did have the spirit, just as Si had said, and just as my brother's dog Shep had had the spirit, too.

*   *   *

Author's Note

I'll tell you, I never knew that the male instinct to protect the young of his species could be this strong. Why, this story about Midnight Duke still gives me chills to this day. Because Duke really wasn't that special in any way and, yet, he really did catch a jackrabbit and climbed over fences and stood guard over mares giving birth. And the day that Duke attacked Diamond, who'd run a mare and her young colt off the water trough, still stands in my mind as one of the greatest feats I've ever seen. I mean, the power with which he did it, the quickness of his decision and action, were absolutely astonishing. But once more, the full impact of this story didn't hit me until years later.

I swear, I sometimes think that our lives really have very little meaning until we've gained some distance, so we can appreciate the things that we've lived through.

Enjoy! Always enjoy! For these times that you might be living through right now might seem confusing and lonely and not make much sense. And yet these might be the very years that you'll look back upon as having been that time in your life that made you the wonderful person that you are!

Walking Stars

We were pregnant. We were expecting our first child. I'd gained twenty pounds and Barbara had gained forty. We were living in the old bunkhouse on my parents' ranch in Oceanside, California, and I was thirty-five and had been writing for fifteen years. I'd written twelve books and sixty-five short stories, but so far I'd only had two sales: a book called *A La Brava*, which my New York publishers had re-named *Macho*, and another book, *Jury*, about the Juan Corona mass murders in northern California.

I figured that I was now a professional and so, maybe, I was ready to do my parents' book. I didn't want our child to go to school and be made to feel ashamed of his or her Indian/Spanish heritage, as had happened to me. But the more I interviewed my parents and aunts and uncles, the more confused I became, because I just couldn't believe any longer in the stories that they told me. And when I tried to skip over my parents and write about my own life in the *barrio* and on the ranch, I found myself having the same problem. I just couldn't believe in those realities of my child-hood anymore either. It was like I'd become cynical, and I doubted that that night of my brother's dog going crazy had ever really happened, or that Midnight Duke had ever really climbed over fences to protect mares while giving birth. These stories just seemed too sentimental, too romantic, too unbelievable.

So, here I was with my father, interviewing him as I baby-sat my son, David Cuauhtemoc, and I couldn't believe the story my father was telling me about this great serpent of Los Altos de Jalisco that had attacked men on horseback, knocking them off their horses.

"And everyone was terrified," my father continued excit-edly, "because the serpent had already eaten several little kids and baby pigs. So the day the serpent attacked your grandfather, Don Juan, he, being a great horseman, ripped a branch off a dead tree and rammed it into the serpent's mouth. Then, he roped the monster and dragged it into town, where some woodsmen chopped off the head."

I wanted to laugh, to burst out giggling, but I didn't, and my dad continued.

"Then the heavens opened up!" said my father, smiling gloriously. "And the people rejoiced and they celebrated for days, for the Devil had once more been beaten by a stout-hearted Christian and God was happy!"

"Oh, Papá!" I said, not able to hold back anymore. "That was a good story when I was a little kid, but I'm a man now, a professional writer, and I can't write that down!" I added, laughing.

"Why not?"

"Because it's not true."

"But I saw the serpent with my own eyes when they dragged it into town!"

"Did it have wings?" I asked sarcastically.

"No, I don't think so," said my father. "But some serpents do, I guess, like that one the Chinese bring out for their parade each year."

"But those are legends, Papá! Not truth."

"Oh? And who says that legends aren't truth?"

I was stopped. "Well," I said, "if they are true, then no one can prove them, and so I can't write about them."

"Then you got real problems," said my father, "because all the most important things of life can never be proven. Like my mother's love and her power when we came off the mountain into the war and all that destruction. How can anyone prove her love, eh, you tell me? Love can't be proven, and you are a fool, and so is all your writing, because these are the real things of life!" He was angry.

"Then you're saying that that serpent truly happened?"

"Of course!" he said. "Absolutely!"

And he went on and on, but I quit listening. I just couldn't understand my parents' world. It was too fantastic, too removed from my modern-day reality.

But then one day, shortly after that incident, Barbara and I were down at the San Diego Zoo with our little son David, showing him the elephants and other animals. Then, we came to all these snakes behind glass, and I suddenly got an idea. It was as if a 120-watt light bulb had lit up inside my head. Quickly, I went looking for the office of the snake department. When I found it, I asked for the main snake handler.

"What do you want?" the lady asked me.

"You know," I said, "I want the person who runs this place and knows all about snake-ology, or whatever, so I can talk to him, or her."

"You can write to our office if you have some . . ."

"Look!" I said. "I need to see this person right now! I have some important information about an unusual snake."

"Oh," said the woman and went to the back.

"Maybe you better go outside, Barbara," I said to my wife nervously. "This might prove embarrassing."

Barbara went out with our son. It was a beautiful, sunny day. Finally, the woman came back with a man who was probably in his mid-fifties. It looked like he'd been eating. He was wiping his mouth and still chewing.

"Sorry to disturb you," I said, "but are you the guy who, well, studied snake-ology, or whatever you call it, and knows all about snakes?"

"Well, to some degree. I have been in the field for . . ."

I cut him off. I was beginning to feel so ridiculous that I knew that I'd chicken out if I didn't speak quickly. "Look," I said, "I've been told . . ." and I didn't say that my father had told me in case it turned out badly, ". . . that, well, there is a snake that can stand up six or seven feet tall and will attack a man on horseback, trying to knock him off his horse so it can eat him."

"Where?" said the man.

He surprised me. He hadn't laughed. No, he'd asked, "Where?"

"Well, in Mexico," I said.

"What kind of terrain is it?" he asked.

"Well, mostly high desert, but in the low places it gets

lush and green, and during the rainy season, it gets to be like jungle all over."

"Sure, that's a bushmaster," he said.

"A bushmaster? You mean, such a snake really exists?"

"Yes."

"But how does a snake get six or seven feet tall?"

"A bushmaster raises up half of its body length. So if it's twelve feet long, it can raise up six feet, and if it's fourteen feet long, it can . . ."

"My God!" I yelled. "Then my father's story is true!" I gripped my forehead in terrible pain.

"Are you okay?" he asked.

"Yeah, sure, I mean, oh, my God! This is wonderful!"

"Do you know the whereabouts of a bushmaster? We could use one for the Zoo."

"Well, no, not yet exactly, but . . . oh, my God! My God!" My mind was reeling, exploding, going crazy. "But, just wait," I said. "Would it attack a man on horseback?"

"Sure, why not? They are fearless. That's why they're nearly extinct. They'll attack a car, a train, anything."

"And could they eat some little kids or baby pigs?"

"Well, yes, a rattlesnake is much smaller, and it eats rabbits."

"Oh, my God, my God!" I yelled, now holding my head with both of my hands. I was erupting inside. Why, I'd been the Doubting Thomas. I'd been the whole problem, not my father, not my mother, and not my childhood memories. It was me!

And so with this incredible breakthrough, I went home and began to interview my parents in earnest and to accept everything they told me, whether I believed it or not. But, still, so much of what they told me I just couldn't commit to paper, because it seemed so foreign to my modern, English-speaking mind that I felt foolish when I tried to write it down.

Finally, I knew that I'd have to go down to Mexico and see things for myself. Because, no matter how open I was now to what my parents told me, I still got stumped by their reality, especially when they used words like "miracles," "angels," "God," "Devil" and *"bruja"* so often that it just seemed ridiculous to my modern-thinking mind. Why, they spoke of each new day as if it were a magical gift from God, a daily miracle of love, offered to us on the wings of angels by the Almighty. And the sun was the Right Eye of God. Boy, it just seemed too flowery and romantic to me, and it really had nothing to do with basic reality, as they kept insisting.

I went by plane to Ciudad Obregón and traveled by second-class bus up to Choix. Next I took a "tran-vía," meaning a tall, five-ton truck with benches in the back, up into the mountains, then floated across rivers on rafts. That first night we slept in La Reforma, a modern-day silver mining town. The next day, we hired an eighty-four-year-old man to guide us afoot up to where my mother had been born, in La Lluvia de Oro.

I had one arm in a cast from a motorcycle accident, but I was in excellent shape because I ran long distances. Still, I was hardly able to keep up with this old man. His name was José María, and he had thirty sons, and he'd known my mother's family well. In fact, he asked how my Aunt Carlota was, saying that she'd had *las piernas más tornadas*, the best-carved legs in all the village.

Then, coming around a bend on the trail, José María suddenly stopped, knelt down and began to pray.

"What is it?" I said to him, coming close.

"No, stay back," he said. "Can't you feel it? This is an unholy place, a violent act was committed here."

"No, I don't feel it," I said. "What happened?"

"I don't know exactly, but someone was killed, that's for sure," he said, and he continued praying.

I glanced around, looking for traces of something violent having occurred. But I saw nothing.

After he finished praying, he got up and we continued. And then, just as we were entering the box canyon where my mother had been born, he stopped on the trail and began to pray again. And he was happy this time.

"What is it?" I asked, coming close again.

"A child was born here," he said. "Can't you feel the miracle?"

"No," I said, "I can't. But miracles can be felt, eh?"

He didn't even bother to answer me. After he finished praying, we went into the canyon and he pointed to the mouth of what used to be a gold mine and then pointed down below, where the village of hundreds of people had once stood. Then we followed the old road into the canyon, and he took me to the boulder where my mother was born and, my God, there was the bolt of iron that my mother had always told me about that had anchored their home. Chills started going up and down my spine as José María told detail after detail of how it had all once been. But, now, as I glanced around, I could see that there was nothing left of the village or the plaza.

"And where are the mighty waterfalls?" I asked him.

"This is the dry season," he said. "They don't run year-round anymore. Now there's not even a trickle until the first rain. But once the rains are here, then the waterfalls still roar," he added with *gusto*.

We went across the canyon to where the American settlement had been, and there were still a couple of old buildings made of stone and the concrete foundations of some other structure. Here, there lived a couple of Indian families who had some goats and pigs.

Then I spotted boxes of files down in a concrete pit where a mother pig had her young. I was told that this was where the Americans had stored their gold bars before shipping them out.

I jumped down into the pit and started going through the boxes of files and saw that they were mostly written in English. Many were typed, and these came from a mining company from St. Louis and out of San Francisco, California. Some of the stationery had the heading of Lluvia de Oro Mining Company. I couldn't believe my luck. Quickly, I started scanning and found some very interesting information. Why, the accounting sheets showed that in the early 1900s, thousands of ounces of gold had been taken out at a time. Sometimes they hadn't even bothered to ship the silver, because they had so much gold.

I asked José María if I could have some of these records. He told me that I'd have to ask the Indians, since they were the ones who'd found them and kept them all these years.

I asked the old Indian who was watching me if I could have some of the records. He said no. I asked if I could buy some of them from him. He said that he had no use for money up here, since there was nothing to buy with it.

"Look," he said, "do you have anything to trade?"

I opened up my pack and brought out a can of peaches, a camera, some clothes, flashlights, and a knife.

He picked up the can of peaches. It had a colorful label. "For these peaches, I will trade!" he said excitedly.

And he weighed my can of peaches in his right hand, and then took that same amount of records with his left, weighing them, too, and handed me the files that he figured weighed as much as my peaches. Oh, I wished that I'd brought more peaches, but there was nothing else I had that he wanted, not even the knife. It was too small, he said.

Later that day, we went back to the rock where my mother had been born and we set up camp. I read over the records that I'd gotten. By then, it was getting dark and I was looking up at the sky, seeing more stars than I'd ever seen in all my life. We were high up in the mountains, hundreds of miles away from any town or city, and the sky seemed so close and truly magnificent. And in the early darkness there were shooting stars here and there, bursting across the heavens. I felt so far away from the twentieth century and everything I'd ever known. Then, suddenly, it happened. It happened as I stood there, gazing at the heavens. I saw my first walking star and it was coming down out of the heavens, right toward us, down low, over there in the sky. I stood in awe, wondering what I was seeing, and then, here came another walking star, and another, and soon here was a whole line of little stars, zigging out of the sky right toward us.

I'd never seen anything like this in all my life, and so I thought that maybe I'd had one tequila too many. Quickly, I called for José María, who was inside the lean-to that we'd set up.

"What's that?" I said, pointing to the walking stars.

"Oh, those are your guests," he said.

"My guests?!" I said, suddenly getting a little frightened, thinking that maybe I'd gone mad. I mean, those records that I'd been reading had taken me into another time. And all day long, walking around with a man who was in his eighties, and could move so quickly that I had a hard time keeping up with him, was mind-boggling. And so, now, what the hell, I had guests coming from the heavens. "What do you mean, 'my guests'?" I asked, a little unnerved.

"Why, the schoolteacher and her students you invited to dinner," he said calmly.

"Oh," I said, suddenly remembering the school that we'd visited over the top of the box canyon by a little ranch community. We'd casually said, "Why don't you come by and join us for dinner tonight?" "But what are they carrying that's so bright?" I asked.

"Pine-pitch torches," said José María. "Each one has their own torch to light their way down the rocky path. That's a pretty steep climb."

"Oh, I see!" I said, laughing. I could now begin to make out the black mountainside and see its jagged form as it reached up into the sky. "You know," I said, still laughing, "for a moment there, as they came over that pass between those peaks, I thought that they were stars, you know, walking stars, coming to us from out of the Heavens."

"But that's what they are," said José María. "They are walking stars."

"Oh, no!" I said, laughing. "You don't get what I mean. I

mean, that for a moment there, for a split second, when they first come over the edge, I couldn't see the mountain, and so I thought that they were really stars from the heavens, see, real stars, and that they were walking toward us."

"But that's what they are," repeated José María. "We're all walking stars."

"Oh, no, you still don't get it," I said to him. "I'm not speaking in metaphors or symbolism. I mean that I really, really thought for a minute there, as they came over the top, that they were really stars walking to us from the heavens."

He looked at me. "What's wrong with you?" he said. "Don't you know that's what we all are? We're all stars that come from the heavens."

"What?" I said. I couldn't understand what he was saying.

He shook his head. "What did they do to you down there in those United States?" he asked. "That's what we all are, walking stars, every one of us. And we all come from the heavens!"

"You're serious?"

"Of course. Didn't your mother tell you, eh, each night when she put you down to sleep, that you're an angel and you would return to heaven in your sleep and rest with *Papito Dios* and come back all refreshed and good in the morning?"

"Well, yes, she did," I said.

"Then, why are you so shocked?" he asked.

"Oh, my God!" I said, grabbing my forehead. I once more looked up toward the black mountain, and I swear that I suddenly saw that, yes, indeed, this teacher and her students did come from the heavens. They were walking stars. We all were, if only we had the eyes to see life, *la vida*, in all its wonder and magic.

"Yes," I said, tears coming to my eyes, "you're absolutely right. My mother did tell me so, every time she lay me down to sleep when I was little. But, well, I'd forgotten. You know, I'd thought it was just a story. Thank you for . . . oh, my God!" I said.

And in that instant, it all came flashing to me: my mother putting me to bed and calling me her *angelito*, and the stories she'd told me in Spanish to put me to sleep, and that I ended up writing about in *Rain of Gold*. My father's stories came reeling to me, too, and I saw that, yes, he, the nineteenth child, had lived a life of incredible power. His mother had also put him down to sleep with stories of magic and wonder.

And, suddenly, there I was, back on our ranch in California, and I flashed on my brother's dog, Shep, and I once more saw him leap off the highest hilltop so he could intercept my brother's soul on its way back to heaven. I flashed on my grandmother dying in the old ranch house in Oceanside and how I'd held onto her hours after she was gone, for I'd seen her soul rise up from her body like in a dream—a memory that I'd completely forgotten until this very moment.

I flashed on Midnight Duke and saw him standing like a sentry by a mare giving birth. I flashed on my father's story of the night he'd taken on the witch and saved his whole family's immortal soul. I remembered the story of my mother and how she'd helped deliver twins right here by this boulder some sixty years before. And then I felt it; I could feel the holiness of the earth I stood upon. I looked to my right and said, "Those twins of the colonel who lived with my mother's family were born right over there, weren't they?"

"Yes," said José María, "that was the bedroom." He smiled and looked at me with a new respect.

Then the schoolteacher and the students came up. It had taken them nearly an hour to come off the mountainside. And we had dinner, and it was wonderful, and then after dinner, she got a guitar and began to sing. The song was *Yesterday*, and she sang it in perfect English, and I'd never heard the song sung with such heart, such beauty, such wonderful feeling.

"Where did you learn that song?" I asked.

"From the radio," she said. She was a beautiful Indian girl in her late teens or early twenties. She was paid by the state and had been up here in these mountains teaching the local kids for nearly a year now.

"Do you know what the words mean?" I asked.

"No," she said.

"Would you like me to tell you?" I asked.

And hearing this question, I'll never forget, she shouted, she yelled, "Oh, no! Please, don't tell me!" She turned her face away from me, raising up her hand to keep the meaning of the words away from herself.

And in that instant I was taken to yet another whole level of understanding. For I could now see that this had been my mother's power and my father's power, too—this awe of words. This was why this young schoolteacher had been able to sing *Yesterday* with such feeling, such heart, because she didn't know the meaning of the words. The words were still a mystery to her; each word was filled with wonder and magic. Just as each word, a long time ago, when humans had first echoed them, must have been filled with an incredible wonder and magic as people tried to express to fellow human beings these enormous feelings that were deep inside of themselves. Why, the word "God" alone must've brought up feelings of unbearable anguish and awe, beauty and longing, feelings of wonderment and magic. But now the word "God" had been used and abused so much that, at best, it was taken for granted or brought up feelings of self-righteousness, or guilt, or confusion.

Oh, my mind was exploding, going a million miles per hour. And I saw that these people up here—where my mother had been born and raised—who were still rooted to the earth, to the stars and the moon, were languaged with Spanish and their local Indian dialects into a world of feeling and touching, of mystery and wonder! And just as a dog can smell what we humans can't smell and can hear what we humans can't hear and can feel what we humans can't feel, the people up here could still feel the awe of each word. And this was why they lived in a reality that I and my English-thinking mind had a hard time of knowing or believing.

Yes, absolutely, José María had felt the unholiness of that place where he'd first stopped to pray that morning. And he'd also felt the miracle of birth at the second place where he'd stopped to pray. And so, Rosa and Emilio had been right when they'd told me that night back in my childhood that Shep had known that my brother was dying. And Si had spoken the truth when he'd said that Midnight Duke was a very special horse and he could've thrown great colts if he hadn't been cut. Why, all of life was special, and magic and miracles were a normal part of living life.

Each new day truly was a miracle, a gift from God. It really, really was, and so was each night. And my parents hadn't been speaking in a flowery language or metaphors when they'd tried to explain all these things to me. No, they'd been speaking in blunt, raw reality. And when my mother had put me to bed, calling me her *angelito*, she'd truly meant those words, that I was in fact her little angel boy, and I was going to go to heaven to sleep with *Papito Dios*.

Why, it was all true! Absolutely true! I'd just been too much in my own head for so long that I couldn't see it. It was like the child who called to her mother, saying, "Mamá! Mamá! Please, come quick and see! A dancing flower has landed on my hand! And it loves me! Come and look! It can fly! It's an angel!"

And the mother, who'd been doing taxes all day long and didn't want to be bothered, still rushed out to see what was going on. But she then said, "That's just a butterfly!"

"Oh," said the child, repeating what she had heard her mother say, "just a butterfly!" And then, that child knocked the insect off herself and never again could see butterflies with magic and wonder again.

And this was what had happened to me once I'd left my mother's side and started school. The wonder, the magic, was ripped away from me. So, in self-protection I became hard and cynical, a Doubting Thomas. But now that was all gone. This girl, this young, beautiful Indian teacher, had just sent me flying backwards into myself. And now I knew as José María had told me, we're all walking stars, each and every one of us. We're angels, just as my mother had always told me.

And, suddenly, I glanced around and the whole world looked so different, so beautiful and full of magic. I looked up at the sky and felt better than I'd felt in years. It was as if I'd finally come home within myself for the first time in a long, long time.

*   *   *

Author's Note

After this experience, I came back home to the ranch in Oceanside, California, and began to write with a power that I'd never known before. It was as if I had wings, as if I'd been reconnected to the main source of life once again. And I'd work until ten or eleven at night, then get up between three and four in the morning, completely refreshed, and I'd have a clarity of mind that was incredible. And now, when my parents spoke to me about angels and God, miracles and magic, it all made perfect sense to me, and I could commit it to paper without any problems.

You see, I didn't leave those mountains the next day. I spent a whole week up there with José María, and I asked him question after question. And each time he spoke, I'd be so impressed with the clarity of his mind. I mean, he was in his eighties and his last child was four years old. And the way he spoke of life, you just knew that life was eternal, and that we were small, lost people here in the United States. Why, he had absolutely no fear whatsoever of getting old or having wrinkles and he, especially, had no fear of death.

"You know," I told him once, "in the United States, people are afraid of getting old and dying. How come you aren't?"

I'll never forget, he took off his hat and wiped the inside of his brim with the handkerchief that I'd given him. "They must be fools," he said, "because dying is returning to God.

Don't you know that once, a long, long time ago, we were all part of God, and we were at peace, but then there was a big explosion of love and we went flying off in little pieces, each of us becoming our own tiny star, and when we die, we return to God, and that's when we wake up . . . and really live?" He shook his head, putting his hat back on, and smiled sadly. "They must be a very unhappy people down there in those United States, poor souls," he added.

And here he was, old and poor and living in such isolation from all the luxuries of the twentieth century, and yet he felt that he was the wealthy one, and all those people "down there in those United States" were poor, deprived souls.

"Well, then according to you," I said, "that's why we're all walking stars; we're all little pieces of that big explosion of love, and now we're on our way back to God."

"Exactly," he said. "And I'm sure that your mother told you all this, if you'll remember—unless she forgot, too—the sun, the moon, all the heavenly bodies, and even this earth, too, are all alive. We're all living-stars, and we're all going back to our home with God. And when you know this, well, how can you not enjoy getting old and dying?" He smiled a beautiful grin. He had two teeth missing, and the space between his teeth had beautiful, smooth, pink gums. "All life loves going home to its nest," he added.

And he said all this so calmly, so matter-of-fact, like he couldn't quite understand why I didn't know. And it wasn't as if he was trying to convince me, or even cared if I believed him or not. It was as though what he was saying was so basic, so natural, that it was beyond him that anyone couldn't see it.

"But how do you know all this?" I asked.

He laughed a great big belly laugh. "Well, how do you know that the sun has risen? You just open your eyes and see its beauty as it comes up. And even if it's raining and cloudy, you still just look around and see its light and feel its warmth. Nothing can fool you; the sun's light is too powerful for any clouds or mountains to hide it. And the power of God is a thousand times more powerful than all the suns in the whole universe!

"Look," he said, standing up and pointing to the heavens, "right up there, just to the side of those stars. That's where the big explosion of love began. God was feeling alone and wanted company, and so He gave a mighty birth to all of us. Don't you feel it? Here, inside of you? Why, I can still feel that great miracle of exploding birth as if it had only happened yesterday."

"Then, this is the answer," I said, "to feel it, here, inside of ourselves."

"Yes, of course," he said, smiling, then beginning to laugh.

"And once we get into these feelings here, inside, then we can feel even miracles?" I asked.

"But, of course. Our feelings are our life," he said, laughing all the more. "Oh, I just don't know what they did to you down there, but now I'm glad I never went to that country when I was young, like so many of our people. You can lose your soul down there if you aren't careful.

"So tell me," he continued, "how is your mother and your Aunt Carlota? Oh, that Carlota had *las piernas más tornadas* in the whole village." He smiled, showing his missing teeth. "It's been years, but I can still see her prancing up and down the pathways. What a looker that Carlota was! Does she still drive men crazy down there? She was quite the flirt up here, you know. But, maybe, you better not tell her what I've said. She might want to come back up here and do me in!"

And he laughed and laughed, truly enjoying himself.

When I got home, I, of course, immediately told my mother and Aunt Carlota what José María had said, and my aunt got angry.

"That dirty old man! I never liked him," she said. "They didn't live in town like us when we were there in La Lluvia. He and his mother lived over the top of the mountain on a little ranch," said my aunt arrogantly, "and his mother was a witch, and a tricky one at that. Imagine," said Carlota, laughing, "she told the people that she'd had a vision of the Virgin Mary, and people came from all around to pay her money to visit the sacred place. Yes, I had good legs, it's true, but I wasn't going to let a witch's son touch them!"

"Who did you let touch them?" asked my mother, having fun.

"Don't you talk to me like that!" snapped my aunt to my mother. "I'm older than you, and you show respect!"

I interviewed my aunt and mother for weeks, and then went back to work. And I was able to write with such power, with such clarity of mind, that I came to realize that, yes, indeed, I had been reconnected with the main source of life, God Himself, and I could now see, feel, and know, that, yes, we all really are walking stars, each and every one of us, on our journey back to the nest of all life.

Thank you. *Gracias.*

Part Two:
Stories of My Mother

First Day of School

For three days and three nights it rained, and the two main waterfalls of the box canyon gushed forth with the roaring sound of water crashing over the rim of the towering wall of mighty rock. The canyon echoed with the water's thunderous sound, and it continued raining steadily every afternoon for fourteen days. Finally, no beast or human could leave their shelter, the water was gushing down between the three cathedral peaks with such power. The force of the two main waterfalls grew to such magnitude that it deafened the ears and numbed the brain.

The boulder behind Lupe's home divided the waters that came down the steep *barranca*, keeping it away from her family's lean-to, and sent it down the rock-laid pathways toward the plaza, where it formed small rivers, shooting through the village toward the creek below which had swollen and overflowed into a mighty torrent of white water as it roared, crashing out of the box canyon, all the way to the Rio Urique six miles below the mountain.

Colonel Maytorena's young soldiers got restless, not being able to work on the new road through the jungle, and so
several of them—who were from the lowlands and didn't
know the way of the mountains—got on their horses and
tried to cross the creek.

They were young spirited men who thought that no little creek could stop them and their great horses of the
Revolution. Yelling defiantly, they whipped their frightened
mounts into the creek, and the gushing waters took them off
the embankment of great ferns like toy soldiers and sent
them cascading with their horses down through the boulders and roaring white water.

One horse managed to climb up on the side of the creek
farther downstream, but the other poor animal went kicking
and whinnying with his rider over the series of short waterfalls below the town, and then off the mighty three-hundred-
foot fall at the end of the box canyon. Neither of the two
young men was ever found, nor was the body of the horse.

The rainy season lessened, raining a couple of hours
every afternoon, and the canyon filled with new green
growth. Then it was time for school to start. Lupe became
very apprehensive. The schoolhouse was inside the American enfencement and Lupe had never been away from home
before, much less inside the American compound. That evening, Colonel Maytorena noticed that Lupe was very quiet,
so he called her to his lap after they'd eaten—Colonel
Maytorena paid Lupe's mother to provide him meals daily.

"What is it, *querida*?" the colonel said to Lupe, bouncing
her on his knee. "You have nothing to worry about."

"School is about to begin . . . and, well, when my sisters went, they used to go together, and I'll be going all alone."

He laughed. "But, my love, the schoolhouse is just across the canyon."

Lupe tensed, realizing that he didn't understand. Across the canyon was as far away as the moon to her. Why, she'd never been away from her mother or sisters before. This was, indeed, one of the most frightening moments of her entire life.

"Listen, *querida*, I'll tell you a story," said the great man, and he held Lupe to his chest and told her of having grown up with his sisters and brothers and many servants in a large white house on a hill surrounded by patios and tall palm trees.

Lupe closed her eyes, listening in rapture as she felt the buttons of his shirt press against her ear and felt his chest go up and down.

"And I remember well the first day I had to go to school, and my mother had the coachman take me in our great carriage drawn by two grey horses, and how I wanted to cry when he left me there. Oh, I was so frightened, looking at the nuns dressed in black, that I broke from the classroom, climbed over the fence, and ran home so fast that I beat our coachman to the gates."

"Really? You did that?" asked Lupe, sitting up attentively.

"Oh, yes," he said, laughing, "and when my mother took me back, I just ran home again. It wasn't until my mother threatened to tell my father that I finally stayed at school. So you see, *querida*, going to school isn't just a frightening experience for you. It's going to be the same for most of the new children, too."

"But I've never been inside the American place before, and the noise from the crushing plant of the mine sounds like the devil himself."

"Look, *querida*," said her colonel, "do you still have the card I gave you?"

"Yes," she said.

"Good," he said. "Because I'm going to ask you to be very brave and do a very big favor for me. Will you do it?"

"Yes, of course," she said, her heart pounding with anticipation.

"Well, I'll be going out again in a few days and, while I'm gone, I want you to be very brave. Very brave. And on your first day of school I want you to take my card to your teacher and ask her to teach you how to read it. Please, this is important. For if you are brave and true, then the other new children will take heart from you and all will go well. Will you do this?"

Lupe could feel her little heart pounding—she was so frightened. But finally she nodded yes.

*   *   *

The morning that school was to begin, Lupe was as frightened as a mother hen who'd just found the scent of a coyote near her nest. Her colonel was gone, and she really didn't want to go to school, but she'd promised her true love that she would, so she had to do it.

After milking the goats and doing her chores, Lupe quickly got dressed and brushed her hair again and again, trying to look her very best.

The sun was a full three fists off the distant horizon when Doña Guadalupe walked her youngest daughter out to the front of the *ramada* to go to school. Lupe was wearing her new floursack dress that Sophia had embroidered with red and pink flowers around the collar and over her heart.

"Here," said Doña Guadalupe, handing her daughter a little basket full of flowers that she'd picked from her potted plants, "take these to your teacher, Señora Muñoz, and remember, *mi hijita*, wherever you go in life, flowers aren't just beautiful, they also have thorns to protect themselves. So always be strong, my love, and proud. Go with God."

"Oh, Mamá," said Lupe, beginning to cry.

"None of that. Doña Manza's daughters are waiting for you. Now go, *mi hijita*."

They kissed and Lupe turned and started down the pathway, stopping to turn and wave to her mother several times before she disappeared.

Arriving at Doña Manza's house, Lupe saw that Cuca and Uva were ready and their older sister Manuelita was telling their mother goodbye. Lupe could see that all three girls wore dresses made from material that had been purchased at the store.

Walking down to the plaza, Lupe and the three girls were met by the town mayor's youngest daughter, Rosemary, and a half a dozen other children. And Lupe couldn't figure out why, but she thought that Don Manuel's finely-dressed daughter, Rosemary, gave her a nasty look.

But then, Lupe quickly forgot about it as they all went out of the plaza, on the path down to the creek, and they started jumping from rock to rock alongside the rapid-running water. The children laughed, and Lupe joined their laughter—truly enjoying herself so much that she forgot all about her shyness.

But then, getting above the rushing water, all the children had to get in single file so that they could follow the steep path, which twisted up through boulders alongside the rushing water. And at this moment, as they lined up behind one another, Rosemary bumped Lupe and almost knocked her into the rushing white water. Lupe was shocked. She now fully realized that Don Manuel's daughter was, indeed, angry with her and wished to do her harm. But she had no idea why.

Continuing up the pathway along the creek, Lupe was careful to stay away from Rosemary. Then high up on the *barranca*, Lupe glanced down the steep hillside and her heart stopped. Way down below them the whole village was bathed in bright golden sunlight. It looked so toy-like that Lupe hardly recognized it. And the part of the village where she lived looked almost nonexistent as it lay hidden among the big boulders and huge oak trees. In fact, she couldn't even see her home, it was so well hidden by the wild peach trees.

"Hurry," said Manuelita. "We all have to walk through the gates together and go straight to the schoolhouse. The Americans don't want us being around the gates."

Quickly, Lupe followed the older girl and her sisters. And once inside, Lupe could see why the Americans didn't want them staying by the gates; wagons and mules were going every which way. The whole place was a beehive of activity. Up ahead, Cuca took Lupe's hand as they walked along behind Manuelita and Uva, crossing a huge barren field. It was also Cuca's first day of school, so she, too, was frightened.

Going across the open granite compound, Lupe saw the six American buildings. They looked long and dark and huge from so close up. But she also noticed that they had no trees or flowers around them. And armed men walked back and forth on their terraces.

Straight ahead was the crushing plant, making a terrible rumble, and from the plant Lupe could see the cables that carried the iron boxes down from the mouth of the dark mine high above them. Two men and a team of mules came rushing by in a hurry. One of the men was shouting orders in a hard, sharp-sounding language that Lupe had never heard before.

Staying close to Manuelita and the girls, Lupe passed by many tall Americans. Some were almost as tall as her colonel. Lupe recognized one American. He was the young, handsome engineer named Señor Scott who was engaged to María's best friend, Carmen. Many of the girls from La Lluvia had married Americans over the years. But it didn't always turn out well. Many of the Americans gave children to these girls, but then they didn't take their Mexican families back home with them when they left the country. There were many brokenhearted, abandoned young women with fair-haired children in La Lluvia because of this. Lupe and her sisters were always told to keep away from the Americans—they were as bad as the *Gachupines*, meaning the Spaniards.

Up ahead, Lupe could see that they were approaching a little white building with a soft yellow palm roof that sat all alone on the edge of a little knoll. There was an open field in front of the little building where children were playing ball. Some of the children were pure Tarahumara Indians. Lupe had never imagined that there was so much open ground inside the American enfencement. Why, it was a whole city in itself, with fields and corrals for their livestock.

Approaching the little building, Lupe saw a tall American woman and her lovely daughter. They both had long golden hair and they were speaking to a pretty, dark, slender Mexican woman.

"That's our teacher, Señora Muñoz," said Manuelita excitedly to Lupe. "And that's Señora Jones, the wife of the man who runs the mine. And that's her daughter, Katie, who also goes to our school part of the year." Manuelita was very proud, telling them what she knew. "Come and I'll introduce you! Señora Jones likes me! She's always lending me books in both English and Spanish!"

Hearing that she was going to be introduced to this American woman, Lupe became frightened. She'd never met an American before. Quickly, she closed her eyes, asking God to please help her not get impregnated, because for as long as she could remember, their mother had been telling them that a girl could get pregnant by just being touched by an *Americano*. But then Lupe remembered her colonel's card and she opened her eyes. "I have to be brave," she said to herself. "I promised."

"Excuse me, Señora Jones and Señora Muñoz," said Manuelita, "but my sister Uva and I would like you and Katie to meet our little sister Cuca and our friend Lupe."

The two women turned to look at Manuelita and the three younger girls. And, Lupe was just going to hand them the flowers that her mother had sent for them and show them her colonel's card, when Rosemary rushed in, pushing Lupe aside.

"Look at my new dress," said Rosemary. "My mother had it made especially for me!"

The two women looked at Rosemary's dress and watched her whirl around for them. Then the bell rang for school to start. Rosemary took Katie's hand and they were off together. Lupe hid her colonel's card behind the flowers. She felt too embarrassed to try to give it to her teacher now.

"Well, excuse me," said Señora Muñoz, turning back to the American woman, "but I have to go inside."

"It was nice visiting with you, Esperanza," said Señora Jones in Spanish. "And I'll send down those new supplies I told you of as soon as they arrive."

"Thank you," said Señora Muñoz, also in Spanish, "that will be wonderful."

Then the bell rang again and all the children stopped playing and hurried inside the little palm-roof building.

Following Manuelita and her sisters inside, Lupe saw that the schoolhouse was a large, long room with long, child-size tables and benches. A large desk with two chairs was at the front of the room. Lupe wondered if her father had helped build the furniture. After all, he was a finish carpenter.

She glanced around and saw that the walls of the room were made of sticks and mud and were painted white. They weren't weathered and brown like the walls of her home. There was a huge earthen *olla*, or pot, for water in the back corner resting in the fork of a big oak tree branch. Lupe loved the olla—it looked so peaceful.

Gently, Manuelita ushered Lupe and Cuca toward the

front of the room. Lupe noticed that most of the boys, who were all young like herself, remained near the rear. They reminded her of rebellious male calves refusing to follow their mother on a path around the mountain.

Lupe knew one of the boys. His name was Jimmy. His father was one of the American engineers who'd married a local girl and then abandoned them. Lupe nodded to Jimmy as she went down the aisle. Jimmy smiled at her. He had large blue eyes, dark hair, and was extremely good-looking. He lived up the *barranca* from them and his home was even smaller and poorer than theirs.

"Lupe, you sit here with Cuca," said Manuelita. "And you help them, Uva. I have to sit up there in front with Señora Muñoz to help her with the lessons."

Lupe pursed her lips together and shuffled her feet, but she said nothing. She sat down, doing as she'd been told, but she didn't like it. She gripped Cuca's hand under the table. Cuca gripped her back. She, too, was scared. Katie and Rosemary came down the center aisle, laughing happily, and sat down directly in front of Lupe and Cuca. They were by far the two best-dressed girls in all the school. Lupe was glad that she'd worn her newest dress.

Then Señora Muñoz came to the front of the classroom and got behind her desk made of fine white-pine. She said good morning to Manuelita, who stood alongside her, then she turned to the class.

"My name is Señora Muñoz," she said, smiling kindly. "I'm your teacher and we'll be working together." As she spoke, she waved her hands about so elegantly, like birds in flight. Lupe was enthralled; all her fears went out of her.

Señora Muñoz was like her colonel: a person who'd come into her life and touched her very soul.

And so everything was going very well until each student had to stand up and introduce himself. Suddenly, Lupe's whole world caved in.

"And we'll start with the first row," said Señora Muñoz. "So, please, don't be shy and, if you're new and get a little bit nervous, please don't worry about it. Someone who knows you will be glad to assist you."

Lupe could have died. She was in the second row. And so, there it came, and Katie got up first and she was tall and confident and poised.

"My name is Katie Jones," she said. "I live with my father and mother in the last building up the hill. My father is Mr. Jones and he manages the gold mine. My mother's name is Katherine and she was a schoolteacher in San Francisco, California, where we have our permanent home on Nob Hill overlooking the Bay. I'm ten years old and this is my second year here in La Lluvia de Oro. But I'll only be here for part of the year. My mother and I have to return to San Francisco for the Christmas holidays. Thank you very much. I'm sure we'll have another fine school year together."

Everyone applauded, saying hello to Katie. She sat down and Rosemary stood up. Rosemary looked confident, too, but there was something different about her.

"My name is Rosemary Chávez," said Don Manuel's youngest daughter, glancing around with a smile, "and my father is the accountant at the mine. He makes the payroll and sees to it that all your fathers, who are lucky enough to work at the American mine, are paid. I live in the largest house down in the main plaza next to the market, which, of course you all know, my father also owns. We have the only home in all the village that has tile in every room. I, too, will not be here for the entire school year. I'll be going with Katie to do the Christmas holidays in San Francisco, where I stayed with Katie and her family last summer to learn English—which, I might add, I speak without accent just as my two older sisters do. Thank you."

And saying this, she sat down, too, and everyone applauded again. Then it was Uva's turn and next it would be Cuca's. Then it would be Lupe's and she was so scared that she wasn't even able to hear what Uva or Cuca said about themselves. Then it was Lupe's turn, but she couldn't even move, much less say anything.

"It's all right," said Señora Muñoz, seeing the young girl's difficulty, "just take your time. Everything is fine."

Lupe sat there staring at the floor, beginning to tremble—she was so frightened.

"Well, then," said Señora Muñoz, "would anyone like to help her?"

"Yes," said Rosemary, quickly getting to her feet, "I'll do it! Her name is Lupe Gómez. She's Carlota Gómez's sister, and they live so high up on the hill that they don't have a real home. They live in a shack and they make their living by feeding miners and taking in their laundry because they have no father and they're so poor."

The shock, the rage, the anger that came bursting into Lupe's heart when she heard these awful lies brought her to her feet before she realized that she'd even moved.

"No!" she screamed. "That's not true!" She was trembling with fear, but she didn't care. "I do have a father! And we do have a real home!" Her heart was going wild. "Rosemary is wrong," she said, tears coming to her eyes. "My name is Guadalupe Gómez Camargo, and my father's name is Don Víctor, and he's a fine carpenter. In fact, he probably built these tables and benches that we're sitting on. But when the American buildings were finished, there was no more work for him, so he went down to the lowlands looking for work. And, yes, we are poor and we do feed the miners and take in their laundry, but our home was built by my father for us with his own two hands, and we have a roof that's good to keep the rain out and walls that block the wind.

"My mother is a fine cook and everyone respects her, and she keeps potted flowers in front of our *ramada* and . . . and . . . she leads us in prayer three times a day, and that's what makes a home!"

And saying this, Lupe burst out in tears, got up from her bench, and took off running down the aisle between the long tables and benches.

Jimmy clapped and whistled. "There, Rosemary," he shouted, "start trouble, and you get the goat's horn!"

"Jimmy," said Señora Muñoz, "you stop that! And Rosemary, I'm ashamed of you. You'll stay after school!"

"But, why? I only told the truth. That's what my father told us!"

"That's quite enough, Rosemary," said her teacher.

"But I did nothing wrong," she pleaded. "I'll tell my father," she added angrily.

"Fine," said the teacher patiently, "but you'll still stay. Now, no more."

Outside, Manuelita caught Lupe before she ran out of the main gates.

"Lupe," said Manuelita, "you did wonderfully! I'm so proud of you. You put that nasty Rosemary in her place and yet you behaved like a perfect lady."

But Lupe wasn't listening to what her friend was telling her. She had the hiccups, and she was looking across the canyon. In spite of her anger, Lupe realized that she'd never before seen the towering walls of rock from this angle. Why, *Dios mío*, the three mighty peaks were even taller and more magnificent than she'd ever known. But looking at them through the wire fence, the cathedral rocks also looked imprisoned.

"Oh, Lupe, I'm so proud of you," repeated Manuelita, and she took Lupe in her arms. "You were brave and good and I love you for that. I want us to be close friends."

And there it began: a friendship, a new kind of love. So Lupe relaxed, letting herself go, and she cried on the older girl's shoulder until she felt all good and clean inside. Why, this older girl had caused their souls to touch, and it didn't really matter to her anymore what Rosemary had said. She had a real friend now, she just knew it. And she'd kept her promise to her colonel, too, and had been brave.

*   *   *

Author's Note

This story has always moved me in a very special way, because as I interviewed my mother sixty-some years after the fact, her eyes would still light up with anger at Rosemary and with joy at remembering her colonel and Manuelita—who later became my Godmother.

"There are many kinds of love," my mother explained to me, "and love really does help us in our darkest hours. And that was one of my darkest—I was so shy and I'd never been away from home. And later I realized why Rosemary was so mad at me and my family. The colonel had selected our home for his wife instead of theirs with tile and wealth. Our town mayor must've been going crazy with jealousy, the poor man."

Also, this story impresses me because it's so timeless. We've all had our first day at school, or on the job, or whatever.

Thank you. *Gracias.*

Wow, I'm proud of my mother.

Woman's Greatest Power

The moon was full and the coyotes were howling and the dogs of the village were barking. Doña Guadalupe decided that she couldn't deliver Socorro's baby alone. The full moon was the most powerful time of the month, and strange things happened to women in labor during this time.

Doña Guadalupe sent Lupe and Victoriano for the midwife while she and her three daughters heated water and prepared for the birth. Lupe and her brother ran up the pathway to the main road and then out of the mouth of the canyon in the bright moonlight.

The midwife's name was Angelina. She and her husband lived just outside of the canyon on a little *ranchería*. They had their home in a small hole nestled up against the mountain.

Scrambling down into the hole, Victoriano called loudly so the ranch dogs wouldn't attack them. Angelina heard them calling and came out to quiet the dogs. At this time of the month, the midwife was very busy. More babies were born during the full moon than at any other time.

The midwife was a full-blooded Tarahumara Indian and she was married to the town drunk, El Borracho, who was the finest guitarist in all the region. There wasn't a family in all of La Lluvia de Oro who hadn't been serenaded by El Borracho at their wedding or helped in childbirth by his wife Angelina.

"Who's in need?" asked Angelina. Her two front teeth were missing and her smile looked like a dark hole in the moonlight.

"The colonel's wife," said Victoriano.

"Oh, she's big," laughed the midwife. "I saw her the other day when I brought your sister María a love note." Angelina was also the local matchmaker who delivered messages back and forth between prospective lovers. "Well, let's go," she said, and she took off at a run.

Going back up into the canyon, neither Lupe nor Victoriano, who were young and good runners, were able to keep up with the old midwife. Once, long ago, when the first Americans had come in from California to work the mine, Angelina had run a foot race against six young engineers who'd said they were great athletes. The distance had been twenty-five miles. She'd been five months pregnant, but still she came in over an hour ahead of all of them.

Arriving at the *ramada*, the old midwife was hardly out of breath. Quickly, she examined Socorro. Then she gave her the heart of a dried cactus to chew—the same kind that the great Tarahumara runners used when they ran a race worthy of a man, meaning a hundred or more miles—and she told everyone to leave the lean-to except for the women who were going to assist her.

"All right, out, *mi hijita*," said Doña Guadalupe to Lupe, ushering her out the door along with Victoriano and Don Benito.

"But, no, Mamá," said Lupe, "I want to stay."

"Let her stay," said the midwife, rubbing an oily liniment into Socorro's legs and feet. "No girl is ever too young to learn the ways of a woman. Believe me, I know. It's the ones who never see who end up having the most difficulties with men and life."

"Please, Mamá," said Lupe, not once taking her eyes off the midwife and the shiny herbal oil she was rubbing into Socorro's limbs. The oily substance smelled good and strong and brush-like. "I want to help. I promised my colonel that I'd care for his wife."

Doña Guadalupe didn't like it, but she was too busy to argue. Socorro was crying out in pain and the coyotes were answering her from the distance. The whole night was full of eerie sounds.

"Oh, all right," said Doña Guadalupe, "but you leave the moment you can't stand it, you understand?"

"Yes, Mamá," said Lupe, and she came close to help her sisters.

They had a lot of work to do. They had to get the big rope tied to the stout center post of their lean-to, heat up water, and help the midwife massage and give comfort to Socorro. A mother in labor had to be kept relaxed so the child would come happily into the world.

Lupe could feel the nervous anticipation inside the dimly lit lean-to as the women went to work. This was a place where no men were allowed; it was only for women. All her life, Lupe had been told that men were weak and simply couldn't endure the pain a woman could.

Outside of the *ramada*, Victoriano sat with Don Benito, looking up at the stars and listening to Socorro's cries of pain.

"I love Lydia," said Don Benito, "but those screams scare me more than bullets."

Two days before, Don Manuel had taken two shots at the old man when he'd come to serenade his other daughter, Lydia, under her bedroom window. The whole pueblo was hissing with gossip about old man Don Benito's courtship with the mayor's daughter, whom the mayor had specially groomed so she could marry an American.

"I'll never do this to my Lydia," said Don Benito. "It's just awful what women have to suffer to bring life into the world."

Inside, the midwife was trying to get Socorro to open her mouth wide and let the pain come out.

"Open your mouth," said Angelina, massaging Socorro's neck and shoulders, "and let out what you feel. Don't keep it in, *querida*. Let it out."

Socorro cried softly at first, but little by little she loosened up and began to let out long, ear-piercing screams.

"Good," said the midwife, "now breathe deeply, deeply, and then cry out again, letting all the pain go out of your body."

Socorro did as told, letting out another cry. Lupe, to her own surprise, wasn't getting upset by the cries. No, she felt relieved. The cries just seemed so natural. But Lupe could see that the cries were making her sister, Carlota, very nervous.

"Good, *mi hijita*, good," said the midwife. "That last one truly came up from here, in your stomach. Now, roll softly side to side. Yes, that's it, and roll out long, soft guttural grunts like a pig. No, don't laugh." She smiled. "The pig is a very good mother, *mi hijita*, and she's also very strong and brave.

"Now, grunt, that's right, grunt strong and deep, and with each sound imagine your body opening up, opening up, larger and larger like a rose, like a flower opening up to the sunlight, like you're going to make love to an enormous watermelon."

Doña Guadalupe didn't like it. Sofía and María blushed. Carlota screeched with embarrassment. Lupe didn't understand. But even Socorro, in the midst of her pain, had to smile. The thought of making love to a watermelon sounded simply awful.

"Oh, you think that's funny?" said Angelina, turning to Carlota, who couldn't shut up. "Well, you young girls just remember what you're seeing here the next time a boy makes eyes at you. For the man, it's only joy. But for a woman, she has to carry the responsibility of that joy and confirm it before God in PAIN!" She yelled out the word "pain," deliberately scaring the young girls.

Doña Guadalupe went to attend to the water on the wood-burning stove across the room. She'd never liked this midwife and her famous tongue. But she was the best midwife in the area, and she'd known Socorro was going to have a difficult time.

The cries of pain continued, and Doña Guadalupe and

María and Sofía helped the midwife massage and comfort Socorro as Lupe and her mother kept the boiling water coming so the lean-to would keep warm and moist. But Carlota wouldn't help. She just stood there, holding her ears, not able to bear Socorro's screams anymore.

And then Lupe smelled something that she'd never smelled before. And the smell got stronger as the cries and groans of pain continued.

But then, suddenly, the cries stopped and a steady rhythm of rolling guttural sounds began—slowly at first, then faster and stronger. And outside, Lupe could hear the coyotes in the distance and the dogs and the goats and cattle in the town. It was a symphony of sound, rolling and growing and echoing off the mighty cliffs.

"Drink, *mi hijita*," said the midwife to Socorro, "you're losing your water."

"No," said Socorro. She was full of pain and wanted to be left alone. But her water had broken, so the midwife insisted.

"Open your mouth," she said, "and do as I say. Drink, drink, yes, that's right, all of it."

It was a specially prepared potion of wild herbs and roots that women took in this region of Mexico while in labor.

Reluctantly, Socorro drank it down. The hours passed and the moon moved across the heavens. The pains of childbirth continued as Socorro's body opened up, bones and flesh moving—one of the greatest miracles in life—opening up like a rose, a flower welcoming the birth of new life. And all the women in the lean-to knew that God, the Father, was here on earth with them, giving them power through the spirit of the Virgin Mary and helping them in their time of need.

And then it was time, and Angelina reached up inside Socorro with her hand, checking the movement of the bones spreading.

"You're ready," said the old midwife. "Your bones have moved, and the baby's in place." The old woman had beads of sweat running down her face. "You're doing good, *mi hij-ita*," she added. "Very good. The spirit of Our Lady is with us tonight. But virgin, she never was." She laughed. "Hell, giving birth to God must have moved more bone than a mountain, I tell you," she said, laughing in her coarse-happy voice. "Now come, Sofía and María, you two help me lift her and put her to the rope so you'll both know how to do this when your time comes."

Sofía and María came forward and lifted Socorro by the armpits, helping her to the thick rope which hung at the center of the lean-to.

"Get hold of the rope," said Angelina.

Lupe could see that it took all of Socorro's power to obey the midwife and grip the rope.

"Now squat," said Angelina, "like you're going to take an enormous *caca*."

María and Sofía laughed.

"Stop that," said the midwife, "and hold her strong so she can squat Indian-style on her haunches. This is the best way for childbearing, and I don't care what the priests or doctors say!"

The old woman now knelt down close to Socorro and massaged her great stomach and buttocks as she told her to begin to push and grunt in rhythm. The young pregnant woman gripped the stout rope and pulled and grunted as she forced down with all her power. And Lupe watched her, squatting there, face straining as if she were constipated, forcing down with more power than she'd ever thought a woman had in her.

"Good, *mi hijita*," said the midwife, "push down and pull on the rope and stare straight ahead and keep in mind only what I'm telling you. Don't fight. Your body and your baby know everything. Good, catch your breath and we'll do it again."

Lupe and her mother brought over another olla of hot water, and the lean-to smelled warm and moist. Lupe could hear Socorro's quick little fast breaths, catching her strength between pushes, and then here it came again, another long roll of forceful grunts as she pushed and pulled.

"Good," said the midwife in her ear, talking so softly that it almost sounded like Socorro's own brain was talking to her.

Then it came again, a series of terrible cries. Then a small hairy, wet spot poked out between Socorro's muscular legs as the midwife talked faster and faster, massaging Socorro's huge stomach with one hand and helping her between her legs with the other.

Lupe froze, staring in disbelief as she watched and heard and felt the power of this miracle of miracles. Her eyes filled with tears.

The head of the baby was now beginning to come out, to appear in the yellow-glow of light of the hanging lantern, and Lupe stood there, huge-eyed with excitement.

But upon seeing the baby's head, Carlota ran out of the

lean-to. "I'll never have children as long as I live!" she screamed.

The midwife had Socorro lean back on the mattress they'd brought up and rest with her legs up and wide apart. Lupe couldn't take her eyes away. She'd never seen a woman in this position before—all hairy and open and wet with the top of the infant's head coming out of her.

Then, having given her blood-gorged legs a rest, the midwife had Socorro squat down once more and grip the stout rope. Pushing and pulling and forcing down with all the power of her young, strong, supple body, Socorro pulled on the rope with her strong young hands and she pushed again and again, long and hard and steady, sweating profusely. The midwife wiped the sweat from her face, and María and Sofía supported her under the armpits while Doña Guadalupe helped the midwife with the baby.

Suddenly, the whole head of the baby popped out, long and lopsided, wet and shiny as a big-headed rabbit, covered with a transparent silvery, slippery mess of non-smelling film. And Socorro now did everything by herself, screaming, pulling, pushing, as if she'd been doing it for ten million years.

And the cries were good, coming from her gut, and her pushes were good, too, coming down with all the power of her young, strong body. Even the baby was helping. He was moving inside the transparent film, fighting for his life. And Socorro cried out so loud that her sounds went up to the mighty cliffs, hitting them, and then they came back down, echoing in a symphony of sound. And the baby came sliding, slipping out between her taut legs like a huge *caca*.

The coyotes went silent and the dogs quit barking. The

goats and mules went silent, too, listening to Socorro's great cries, now echoing off the mighty cliffs.

Then it was done, just like that, and Lupe was amazed at the nearly odorless smell that filled the room. With all the blood and flesh and slimy liquid that had come out of Socorro, Lupe had expected a much stronger odor. But then she remembered that women up here in the mountains always drank a lot of herbs during their pregnancy.

Holding the newborn up high in the dim light, the midwife now stretched out the twenty-inch cord from the baby's belly to the placenta and gently took it in her hand.

"Look," she said to the three young girls helping her, "you can see life passing through the cord if you look closely."

Drawing close, Lupe saw it was true. She could actually see the cord pulsating with life between Socorro and the child. But then, like magic, the flow of life quit going between the mother and the child. Lupe watched the midwife clip the cord with her mother's sewing scissors. Quickly, she tied the cord, next to the baby's stomach with a string, then put the baby to his mother's warm, soft flesh. Quickly, the child hugged in close, instinctively trying to find a nest as warm and moist as the one he'd just left.

María and Sofía helped the midwife lay Socorro down on their mother's straw mattress. Doña Guadalupe began to wash the child off with warm, clean water as he hugged in close, smelling and getting to know his mother—his first full contact in the world.

Doña Guadalupe put the baby's little feet in a bowl of warm water, and the child continued clinging to his mother. He never cried. He listened to her heartbeat, the same music that he'd heard from inside the womb. No, he was quiet, content, doing what nature had taught him to do since prehistoric times—to keep quiet so the coyotes and other predators wouldn't find him.

Looking at Socorro with her child, Lupe had never seen a more exhausted yet happy-looking woman in all her life.

"Come," said the midwife, "let's leave them alone."

Lupe followed her mother and sisters and the midwife out of the lean-to. Outside, the old woman stretched her tired limbs and caught her breath. Lupe and her mother and sisters joined her, stretching and looking up at the stars and the full-moon night.

"This one, your youngest," said the midwife, turning to Doña Guadalupe as she stretched and worked the small of her back, "is going to be a fine woman. Why, Lupe was sniffing the air, she so much wanted to get into the birth.

"Now, please give this old woman a drink, Doña Guadalupe," continued the midwife, "and let's take a little rest, because in a few moments, the next baby will be coming."

"Another?" said Sofía and María at the same time.

"Yes," said the old woman, "another."

Quickly, Doña Guadalupe went and got the bottle of tequila she kept hidden in the kitchen. She had a drink along with the midwife. Lupe was shocked. She'd never seen her mother drink alcohol before.

Then, they were just catching their breath when there came a new series of cries from Socorro.

They all hurried back inside.

*   *   *

The light of the full moon was dancing off the towering mighty cliffs when Lupe and María came out of the lean-to each holding a child. Victoriano came rushing up with Don Benito and Carlota. They saw the two little infants in Lupe's and María's arms. They were overwhelmed by the miracle of life.

The newborns were moving, squirming, reaching out for *la vida*. It was truly a sign from God. Up in her pen, the mother goat smelled the excitement and called out. The dogs began to bark once more, and the coyotes answered them. Then, the cattle and mules came in, too, and the canyon filled with a symphony of sounds. Carlota forgot her fears and came to María and took the child. Lupe gave the other to her brother.

Lupe and her mother and sisters and brother stayed up the rest of the night with the midwife, talking and drinking and warming their feet on a shovel-full of hard-wood hot coals in front of the ramada. The stars and the moon kept them company and the hard-packed earth in front of the ramada felt good under their bare feet.

Lupe sat there with her mother and sisters as Socorro and her two little boys slept in the lean-to, and she listened to the talk and laughter of the women. The midwife poured tequila in her hot-good herbal tea and told story after story of the different children she'd delivered who were now adults in the community. And it felt good being included by these women into the mystery of life. Lupe felt more complete inside her deepest self than she'd ever felt before.

Then, the eastern sky began to pale. It was the coming of a new day. They all got up to stretch so they could go to work. But instead of feeling tired, Lupe felt refreshed and strong.

"Let us pray," said Doña Guadalupe, and they all knelt down.

And as they prayed and Lupe saw the eastern sky growing yellow and rose and pink, she felt herself fill with such power, with such a strength and well-being, that she just knew in her bones that life was eternal.

Her eyes filled with tears, feeling so close to these women. The whole world sang and danced before her very eyes, and the cycle of life, *la vida,* continued and the new day came forth—a miracle of life, of birth coming from out of the darkness, just as they'd witnessed the miracle of life coming from between a woman's strong, young legs. Life really was eternal. And they, the women, were at the center of it all.

*   *   *

Author's Note

My Aunt Carlota was true to her word, and she never had any children. This birth scene, this night of power and magic, truly put into motion many things deep inside my mother Lupe's soul and everyone else's involved.

What if every young girl, before puberty, participated in a hands-on childbirth? Why, these young women would grow up having a completely different point of view toward sex and life and death and pain and immortality. What if boys participated, too, helping their own mothers and sisters? These boys would grow up having a deep respect for women and sex and life. Why, they'd be completely different adult men and husbands.

Also, please notice how the animals and the night and the moon were participants in the birth. This I saw happen in the village of La Reforma, and that night I came to truly understand that we're all interconnected, if we only have the eyes to see and the ears to hear and the heart to feel.

By the way, this birth scene took me six months to write and sixty-some rewrites and dozens of interviews, not just with my mother and aunts, but with several midwives and Indian women who lived in that region of Mexico. Also, I forgot to put in the story that Indian women used to cook up the afterbirth and feed it to the mother, because it gave her incredible strength and gave her child—through her milk—complete immunity for the first few months.

Thank you. *Gracias.* Boy, did I sweat on this one!

The Hanging

The sun was high overhead and Lupe's brother Victoriano was several hundred feet below the crushing plant of the mine. He was going through the mountain of waste that the Americans dumped down the *barranca*. He was bent over, going through the rock, stone by stone, looking like a tiny ant among the huge pile of waste that had accumulated over the last decade.

He was working and sweating fast. He was looking for the richest rock he could find so that he and his family would have something worthwhile when he took it home and they broke it down with their hammers.

Suddenly, Señor Jones, who ran the mine, appeared above him. La Liebre and two of his gunmen were at his side, smoking cigars and looking very well-fed, compared to when they'd come into the canyon a few weeks back, looking like starving, ragged revolutionaries.

"Hey, you, down there! What are you doing?" shouted Señor Jones.

Victoriano glanced up and saw all four men. His heart took off. *"Nada,"* he said, "just looking through the rock you threw away, hoping to find a little color!"

"Get his basket and bring it up here to me," said Señor Jones to one of the gunmen.

Quickly, a gunman went down the hillside through the broken sharp rock. La Liebre raised his bullwhip, signaling his other gunman to go down, too.

Victoriano didn't know what to do. A part of him felt like running. But another part of him knew that he'd been doing nothing wrong. People had been searching among the waste ever since he could remember.

"Bring him up!" yelled La Liebre to his men. "I think I've seen this one before."

A chubby red-headed soldier grabbed Victoriano, shoving him up the hillside through the broken rock. This was the same red-headed soldier who'd abused a twelve-year-old girl the week before. He was second in command after his captain, La Liebre.

"Well, well," said Señor Jones, looking through Victoriano's basket as the two soldiers stood by him. "What do we have here? This is pretty good ore. Tell me, boy," he said with his Texas drawl, "you got some deal with someone in the mine to throw you out our first-class rock?"

"No, of course not," said Victoriano.

But then, glancing about and seeing their faces, Victoriano saw it coming. Nothing he could say would stop these vicious men. Why, they were sneering at him like huge, hungry cats ready to pounce on a mouse.

"But it's true!" cried out Victoriano. "I worked hard to find these rocks. Please, come down and I'll show you!"

But he saw Señor Jones nod to them and he knew it was no use. They'd made up their minds before they'd ever come down to get him. Suddenly, smiling happily, La Liebre stepped in, hitting him in the stomach with the hard handle of his whip.

"All right," he said to Señor Jones as Victoriano doubled over in pain, "we'll take it from here."

Catching his breath, Victoriano turned and ran, leaping over the broken rock as he sailed down the steep hillside. But he'd gone only three strides when La Liebre leisurely caught him by the ankles with the crack of his bullwhip. Victoriano went face-first into the rock, cutting up his face and hands. Red blood ran down his face and white cotton shirt.

"Get him to his feet!" ordered La Liebre, grinning.

The two armed men ran down and jerked Victoriano to his feet, pinning his arms behind his back.

Smoking lazily, La Liebre came up and looked into Victoriano's young, handsome face.

"We're going to make an example of you, boy," he said. "Brand you and then hang you." And saying this, he took the big cigar out of his mouth and rammed it into the boy's face.

Screaming, Victoriano tried to jerk his face away, but the two armed men held him fast.

"And now to hang you, *muchacho*," laughed La Liebre, realizing that he'd been just about this boy's age when his mother and sisters were killed and he had been disfigured. "We got to show the people what happens to a thief!"

They took Victoriano down through the waste and dragged him across the creek to the plaza.

Señor Jones went back to the crushing plant and took

the main road around the canyon so he could watch without seeming to be involved.

*   *   *

Lupe was in the back of Doña Manza's bakery, doing her studies with the rest of the children when she heard the bell tower down in the plaza. The ringing of the bell was normally a sign of celebration, if there wasn't some catastrophe going on. And so, Lupe and the other children hurried around the stone building with their teacher to see what was going on. Suddenly, she saw some men throwing a rope into the tree above her brother's head, preparing to hang him.

Lupe let out a scream, putting her hands over her face in horror.

"Run!" said Señora Muñoz to Lupe, recognizing Victoriano, too. "Get your mother! Doña Manza and I will see what we can do!"

Lupe was off like a shot, racing past Señor Jones, who was lighting a fresh cigar in the shade of a tree as she went flying up the pathway to her home.

"Mamá! Mamá!" screamed Lupe, rushing into the kitchen. "They're hanging Victoriano in the plaza!"

Doña Guadalupe was at the stove. She'd been putting together what little bits and pieces she had, trying to assemble a meal for the miners tonight. "Who? What are you talking about?" said her mother, seeing Lupe's terrified face.

"Victoriano!" wailed Lupe in terror. "La Liebre is going to hang him!"

Doña Guadalupe dropped the huge kettle and stared at her daughter in disbelief.

Then she was moving, doing, not asking another single

question. And she rushed into the lean-to, all her blood pounding through her body and exploding in her head.

"Quick," she said, ravaging through her wooden chest, "run down to the plaza and get Don Manuel to stall them. Tell him that I'm coming to give my son his final blessing!"

"Yes!" yelled Lupe, running back out of the lean-to, through the ramada, and flying down the steep hillside in great leaps.

Finding her father's gun at the bottom of the chest, Doña Guadalupe took a deep breath. The man who'd raised her and whom she'd called "father" for over thirty years had been the greatest, bravest man she'd ever known.

She'd never forget as long as she lived the morning that their destinies had crossed. She'd been nothing but a child, just starting to talk, and at daybreak the soldiers had hit their encampment, setting fire to their homes and shooting her people, who were Yaqui Indians, as they'd come screaming out of their huts.

Her parents were shot and left to bleed to death. Their home was leaping in flames. Her hair had caught fire and she'd come out of hiding from behind her mother's dead body. She'd asked God for help and had run out of the door, straight toward her enemy with open arms.

The-Man-God-Sent-Her turned and saw her. He was just going to lower his rifle but instead whirled about and shot the soldier right next to him who'd taken aim on her.

Then The-Man-God-Sent-Her got a blanket and smothered the fire in her hair. And while the slaughter continued, he mounted a horse and took off with her. They rode night and day, and when one horse dropped, he stole another.

Getting to his house, The-Man-God-Sent-Her packed

his wife and children and they all fled into the night. They set up residence in a new town, high in the foothills. She was renamed Guadalupe and raised as his own child.

Remembering all this in exploding flashes inside her mind's eye, Doña Guadalupe now checked her father's pistol, making sure that it was loaded. Then, she calmly got her black shawl, placing the pistol underneath, up inside the armpit of her dress.

Taking a big breath, she picked up her Bible and rosary and got a small knife from the kitchen, putting it under her Bible before going out of the lean-to.

People had already begun to gather outside the *ramada* to give her their condolences, but she didn't see them as she passed by. She was of one heart, one mind; she was a mother, a woman, concentrated down to the marrow of her bones on doing one thing, and nothing—absolutely nothing—could distract her, not even death itself.

And there she came, short and plump, walking quickly down the rocky trail that zigzagged between the houses. And *la gente* saw her coming, and they moved aside.

In the plaza, Doña Guadalupe saw that they had her skinny little son under the tree with a noose about his neck. She could also see that they'd abused him—he had so much blood running from his face and the front of his shirt. It took all her power to not cry out in pain and rush up to her baby boy.

But remembering The-Man-God-Sent-Her, Doña Guadalupe held herself strong and continued with all the dignity she could down the steep steps into the plaza itself.

Her daughters were being held back by a dozen soldiers,

and Don Manuel was arguing with the monstrous-faced man as she came through the crowd.

Soldiers were everywhere. Señor Jones was over to the side, smoking a cigar. This was going to be much more difficult than she'd expected.

"Here she comes now, for God's sake!" shouted Don Manuel, seeing Victoriano's mother coming through the crowd.

"All right," said La Liebre. "She can give him her last blessing, but then no more! He hangs, and that's final!"

Seeing her mother, Lupe got down on all fours to crawl under the soldiers' legs who were holding her and her sisters back with the crowd. But one of the soldiers saw her and grabbed her by her hair, jerking her back so viciously that Lupe felt the skin pull away from her eyes.

"Don't you do that again!" said Sofía, grabbing Lupe in her arms. "All we can do now is pray for a miracle, *mi hij-ita.*"

"Mamá will save him!" screamed Carlota. "I know she will!"

María was holding Carlota in her arms. Esabel was standing behind María, giving her comfort.

Don Manuel was still arguing, trying to prove to the people that he was a just man and that he wasn't a pawn of the American company.

And all this time, Señor Jones stood over to the side, joined by a couple of his young engineers. One was eagerly setting up his camera to take pictures.

And then out came El Borracho, getting up from behind the huge tree in which they were going to hang Victoriano.

He'd been asleep in a drunken stupor the whole while. Glancing about, he couldn't figure out what was going on.

Doña Guadalupe rushed forward. She was just about to hug her son when the man called The Jack Rabbit stepped in front of her.

"Wait!" he said. "What do you got there with that Bible?"

"My rosary," she said.

"Let me see," he said.

"No, let her be!" yelled Don Manuel. "Haven't you done enough?"

"You better shut up, old man," said La Liebre, turning on the mayor. "We caught him with the gold!"

As they spoke, Doña Guadalupe rushed to her son, hugging him, covering him with her shawl and whispering in his ear. But Victoriano was so far gone that he didn't recognize her, much less understand what she was saying.

Doña Guadalupe cried out in grief, pretending to lose control.

La Liebre could see that the crowd was getting louder and his men were having a hard time holding them back. People were coming out of everywhere—on rooftops, over walls—and they outnumbered his men sixty to one.

"All right," said La Liebre. "To show I'm a fair man, she can give her son her blessing. But then no more!" He drew his revolver. "The law must be respected! He's a thief and he must hang!"

Hearing this, El Borracho laughed and turned his ass-end toward the many-scarred leader, lifting his right leg and letting out a tremendous fart.

"This is what I think of you and your law!" said El Borracho, cranking his ass around and around, farting all the while. "You don't do crap unless Señor Jones pulls your rope. You ugly abortion of the Devil!"

Everyone in the plaza heard his words, and they were just going to laugh when La Liebre brought up his pistol and fired once, twice, three times, sending El Borracho's body jerking forward with each shot.

Blood and foam boiled out of El Borracho's mouth as he came to rest in a sitting position, eyes still staring in shock.

Silence fell over the plaza. No one so much as breathed. But then *la gente* were screaming, bellowing, raising their fists in anger. El Borracho was one of their most beloved people. He and his wife had brought their children into the world and had sung and danced at their weddings.

And at this moment, Doña Guadalupe took her knife from under her shawl, trying to cut the rope between her son's two fists. But Victoriano's hands were tied so close together that she couldn't get the blade between them.

"Turn your wrist," she said. "Quick, we don't have much time!"

But Victoriano didn't move his wrists and so, out of desperation, Doña Guadalupe took his ear between her teeth, biting and twisting with all her might.

He opened his eyes wide with pain. Suddenly, he saw his mother and realized what was going on. His mother told him what to do again, and this time Victoriano understood her words and his mind came reeling to the present.

He turned his wrists. He could feel her cutting. But they'd tied him up with a twisted rawhide rope and it was tough cutting.

Then Victoriano saw La Liebre coming toward them, reloading his pistol.

"All right," said La Liebre, grabbing Doña Guadalupe by the shoulder. "That's enough! Get away from there!"

The people screamed, yelling for La Liebre to let her finish her blessing. Their roar was so great that the many-scarred man lifted his arms, saying all right.

"Mi hijito," Doña Guadalupe whispered, "I have a gun under my shawl. And as soon as you're free, I'll give it to you. Then I'll leap back, screaming. And you run to the creek." She was cutting the final strand. "Understand, *mi hijito*, I'm not cutting you free so you can be brave and get killed. I want you running so you can live. You run, you hear me? You run for the creek when I jump back."

His hands were suddenly free.

"Don't move yet," she said. "Work your hands. Get circulation into them. I love you, remember that."

He did as told. And she could see that his eyes looked alert now. She felt he was ready. "Here's the gun. Take it. I love you, *mi hijito*. I love you with all my heart. Run when I leap back!"

And she leaped back with her arms stretched up toward the sky, giving him cover as she screamed to the heavens, "God be with you, my son!"

But it was all for no good. The man called The Jack Rabbit had been through many battles. So, when he saw the old woman leap back with arms stretched up toward the heavens, he drew his gun, knowing it was an escape, and rushed in, knocking her out of the way.

And, in that split moment just as he was turning to run, Victoriano saw the man of lightning reflexes come racing behind his mother, and he stopped. He stopped and crouched, spinning about, fully realizing that he could never get away from this man who was so fast. He fired over his mother's shoulder just as La Liebre's ugly face suddenly appeared before him.

The man's face exploded with red blood and pieces of white bone, and then Victoriano was running, shooting into the air as he ran, drawing the soldiers away from his beloved mother.

People scattered—soldiers and civilians alike. Lupe and her sisters broke from the crowd, rushing to their mother as half of the armed men chased after their brother.

But Victoriano was gone, racing through the thick foliage below the plaza, jumping over rocks that he'd known all his life. Then he leaped into the water, going over the series of short waterfalls where the roaring white waters went down to a steady blue flow.

The soldiers fired a few quick shots at his turning, twisting, swimming body, but then quit the chase and went back to the plaza.

When they got back, they found the courtyard full of people. The chubby red-headed man was in charge now that La Liebre was dead. He'd arrested the old woman and the mayor.

"But I didn't know she had a gun!" shouted Don Manuel as they dragged him and Doña Guadalupe across the cobblestones.

Under the big tree, the soldiers put a rope around the necks of the mayor and Doña Guadalupe. But the people had had enough; they were willing to die so the mayor and Doña Guadalupe could live. They came pouring through the armed men like rain through an open hand—mobbing the walkways and climbing over rooftops and stone fences by the hundreds.

Señora Muñoz brought all her children under the tree where they were preparing to hang Doña Guadalupe and Don Manuel. She sat down with them on the cobblestones and they began to sing.

Doña Manza and her family joined them and so did Don Manuel's family. The rest of the people understood what was happening and they carpeted the plaza with their bodies, packed so closely together that the soldiers couldn't move, much less throw the rope up into the branches to do the hanging.

The singing of the people filled the canyon with sound, traveling up to the mighty cathedral rocks and coming back down in an echoing symphony of power and strength—a raw naked force.

Señor Jones was the first one to realize what was happening, and he threw his cigar down, quickly leaving.

Then the red-headed leader glanced about, trying to figure out how he could get out of the plaza before they ripped his weapons away from him and beat him to death. He took the rope off of Doña Guadalupe's neck and fled. The other soldiers quickly followed him.

The people saw the fear in the soldiers' eyes as they fled—fear that they'd been feeling themselves all their lives—and it gave them heart. They raised their voices all the more.

Well over five hundred men, women and children were singing. Their united voices drowned out even the great thundering noises of the American gold mine company.

The miners quit their labor and stood up to listen. Then they dropped their tools to go see what was happening with their families down in the village.

Lupe and her sisters hugged their mother, weeping with joy, and a great flock of parrots—green and yellow with touches of red and blue—came swooping down over the village from the towering cliffs, squawking nervously and looking like angels.

All that night, the Americans slept with guns at their sides for the first time since the Revolution had begun. Soldiers, they'd always been able to handle in one way or another, but this was something entirely different.

The moon came out and the coyotes howled, and *la gente* remained together like the knot of a coiled rattlesnake far into the night. They'd won, they'd won, and they were full of heart.

*   *   *

Author's Note

Interesting, but my mother and aunt didn't remember this story very well. It was my Godmother Manuelita who remembered it best. And she explained to me that Mr. Jones didn't show his true colors until his wife and daughter had left for California. "In fact," said my Godmother, "if his wife and daughter had stayed, I'm sure that the whole thing never would have happened."

This, then, is the story of women, of a school teacher and the bravery of a mother, and then the real power of the people when they finally got together. The heroes of the movies, with their big muscles and big guns and bombs, don't do it in real life. In real life, it's us—me and you. We become the heroes when we finally decide that we've had enough and unite, gaining such power that we can do anything. The battles of life have always been fought by the people, and not just the men, either. Women are tough, too.

I tell you, I still get chills when I think of all their singing voices, uniting and echoing off the tall cliffs and making the parrots take flight. Why, those parrots must've truly looked like angels, and it really must've felt like the heavens had opened up and were smiling down upon them . . . beautiful! Absolutely beautiful!

Part Three:
Stories of My Father

The Greatest Christmas Gift

It was the week before Christmas, and everyone was going crazy around the house. Juan's older sister, Luisa, was going to get married right after Christmas, and much had to get done. So many things had to be accomplished for the holy day of Christ's birthday and then, also, for the wedding. Oh, it was an exciting time at the Villaseñor household in Los Altos de Jalisco.

And this night, right after dinner, Domingo got up and went out the back door, signaling for his younger brother Juan to follow him. But Juan didn't want to go outside with Domingo. No, he wanted to stay indoors with *la familia.* So, Domingo made a face at Juan that said, "You better get out here quick or you're going to get it later when nobody's around to protect you."

Juan took a big breath, glanced around at everyone, and decided that there was no way to escape this. So, he got up and went out the back door, too.

Immediately, Domingo grabbed Juan once they were

out of sight from the adults and gave him a sharp knock on the head with his middle knuckle. "Come on, *cabezón!* They're waiting for us by the creek behind the pig pen!"

Getting to the creek, they met Lucha.

"Where have you two been?" she said. "I slipped out the front door when no one was watching, and I've been waiting for you."

"Is Emilia coming?" asked Domingo.

"No, you know how she is. She's a coward."

"Yes, just like chicken here," said Domingo. "I had to knock him on the head to straighten him out."

Saying this, Domingo went to hit Juan on the head for good measure again, but Juan ducked away.

"Stop hitting me," he said, "or I'll just run home and tell José or Emilia!"

"Oh, you think we're afraid of them?" said Lucha. "I'll show you!" And she took a swing at Juan's large head, but he dodged, knocking her hand away.

Suddenly, a pig squealed an ear-piercing screech right behind them, taking them all by surprise. Lucha and Domingo stopped picking on Juan, and they turned to see the whole pen come alive with squealing, grunting pigs. The dogs at the house yelped and the neighbor's dogs began to bark; a coyote family answered in the distance. The full moon slipped behind a soft, white-laced cloud, giving the whole night an eerie feeling.

"What is it?" whispered Lucha.

"Probably nothing," said Domingo, "or it could mean that those coyotes are a lot closer than they sound."

"Oh, I don't like this," said Juan, glancing around at the night. "Couldn't we wait and do it some other night?"

"No!" said Domingo. "You know that this is the last night of the full moon, so you must do it tonight!"

Juan gulped. "But why?" he asked. What they wanted him to do was go to José-Luis' house and summon the Devil, because they all thought that Luis' mother was a witch. "Wouldn't it make more sense to wait until La Bruja's powers weakened so that I'll have a better chance of doing it for sure?"

"Eh, he has a point there," said Lucha. "We don't want to fail. Our entire family's future depends on this, so maybe it would be best to wait."

"Lucha!" said Domingo, becoming as indignant as an enraged priest, "have you forgotten everything we've been taught at church? The Devil is strong, remember? At one time he was God's most glorious angel, and if we expect to show him that we are not afraid of him, then we can't do it when a witch is at her weakest. No, we must do it when La Bruja's power is at its greatest! Then, and only then—like the good priest says—do we break the evil spell that has been put upon our family."

"Oh, I see. I remember now," said Lucha. "So," she added, shrugging her shoulders, "there is no other way, Juan. You must do it tonight."

Juan's whole body shivered with fear as he glanced up at the bright, full moon and then across the little creek to the far side of the valley. In the distance he could see the tiny light of José-Luis' house and his mother's orchard of peach trees over to one side. His little heart was pounding. He took a big breath. "Look," he said, "maybe the whole wedding will be called off and then we don't even have to worry about having a witch in our family."

"Oh, no, you don't! You started that whole business last night," said Domingo. "And you heard what Luisa said to-night. She and Luis are in love, and the date is set for their wedding. This is the last full moon in which we can save our immortal souls," added Domingo, sounding just like the priest who came to their village once a month.

Juan and Lucha made the sign of the cross over themselves. Domingo really had a way about him.

"Look," said Lucha, drawing close to Juan, "if I could do it for you, little brother, you know I would. But I can't. I'm older than you and not pure of heart anymore, and so it would mean nothing for me to go and confront La Bruja."

Juan brushed Lucha's hand away. Of all his sisters, Lucha was the one who Juan trusted the least. She had big beautiful eyes and was always flirting and acting all lovey-dovey to get her way. He knew that she would no more do for him what had to be done than a fat pig give up his food for another fat pig.

"So, why aren't you pure of heart anymore?" asked Juan.

"Oh," she said, acting like some great lady. "What kind of a man are you to ask a lady a question like that?"

"A boy," said Juan. "A very scared boy who doesn't want to go to the witch's house for all the money in the world. And you're older, Lucha, stronger, faster, and so I want to know why you can't do it."

"Well, if you must know," said Lucha, playing with a long strand of her hair, "Last summer I . . . but you must swear to never tell a soul!"

"We wouldn't!" said Domingo excitedly. "I swear it! So come on, tell us," he added quickly.

"Well, ah," she said, smiling and looking at them from the corner of her eyes, "you know our cousin Agustín. Well, when he stayed with us, he and I, well . . ." she turned all red. ". . . we kissed."

"You kissed Agustín?!" said Domingo. "But he's our first cousin! How could you do such a thing?"

"Well, we just kissed. It's not like we're going to get married or have a baby."

"You better not!" said Domingo. "It would have a long pointed tail, because it would be a baby conceived of the Devil!"

"I know. That's why we only kissed, but by the hours," she added, laughing.

"You . . . enjoyed it?" asked Juan.

"Yes, very much," said Lucha.

"Eeeuuuuu!" said Juan, making a face of pure repulsion.

Lucha went to hit Juan, but Juan only laughed and dodged away. "I'm going to brain you!" she said.

"Enough! Stop that! Both of you!" said Domingo. "What we have here tonight is VERY serious. It's about saving the immortal soul of our entire Villaseñor family."

Juan and Lucha immediately settled down, because they both knew that Domingo was right. Ever since José-Luis had come to their home and asked for their sister Luisa's hand in marriage, the other kids in the village had been telling Juan and the other younger kids of his family that they were now all destined to go to hell. For everyone knew that Luis' mother was a witch of the highest power. And when her son married into the Villaseñor family, then Luis' mother would also be part of the Villaseñor family. They'd all be condemned to burn in the fires of hell for all eternity.

"All right now, do you remember what you're supposed to do?" asked Domingo of Juan.

Juan nodded. "Yes, I remember."

"Well then, repeat it. I don't want any screw-up."

Juan lowered his head, feeling like he might cry. "I'm supposed to go up to her house and . . ."

"I can't hear you! Talk louder! And look at me in the eyes, like a man!"

Juan lifted his face. His eyes were brimming with tears. He was just a scared little boy, but he straightened up the best he could, trying to look like a man. "I'm supposed to go up to her house," he repeated, "then say aloud that I don't fear her powers or the Devil's, either, then . . . then . . ."

"Then what?"

Juan's eyes became huge. "I'm supposed to make the sign of the cross and yell 'We walk in God's love and we fear no evil!' "

"Exactly," said Domingo, "exactly."

"But—but—but what if her five big dogs wake up?" asked Juan. "Maybe I should just whisper it and not say it out loud." He had to squeeze his legs together so he wouldn't pee. "That huge black dog, the one called El Diablo. Oh, my God, if they wake up, they'll kill me and eat me! You saw what they did to that stranger last year. They took him down, with his horse, too, and half-ate him before she could call them off."

"We've been over that!" snapped Domingo impatiently. "That's why you circle her house, coming in through the peach orchard. Her dogs sleep on the other side of her house. They won't even hear you, if you do it right."

"Oh, Domingo," said Juan, his little heart going crazy, "why can't you do it for me? I'm scared and not as fast or as strong as you."

"Look, *cabezón*, we've been over this a dozen times! I'm older than you and not pure of heart anymore! You know that! I'm mean to you and kick dogs and torture ants and swear all the time!"

"Look," said Juan, "I'm not so pure, either. I've kicked goats and tortured bugs, too. And last year when the priest came and found the poor box empty at the church, it was me who took the money."

"You took that money?!" yelled Lucha. "How awful! And you never spoke up when the priest kept accusing us all of stealing! That was terrible!"

Domingo looked at his little brother with new respect. "You really did that?" he asked.

"Oh, yes," said Juan, "and I've done other bad things, too!"

"Like what?" asked Lucha.

"Well, I've sneaked up and watched how you girls have to squat down to pee, and we don't."

"You've watched us?!" yelled Lucha. "Oh, you're dirty!"

"No, I stand up to pee," he said proudly.

"I'm going to hit you and tell Mamá!" yelled Lucha, grabbing Juan and trying to hit him on the head. But he kept ducking. Domingo separated them.

Just then, some other kids came running up. It was Mateo, Domingo's best friend, and his two smaller brothers, Alfonso and Pelón, and their sister Carmelita. Immediately,

Mateo wanted to know what was going on. He and Domingo were the two best fighters with rocks or their bare hands in all the region. They were so feared that even some adult men wouldn't go against them in an all-out rock fight.

"My little brother is ready to do it," Domingo announced proudly.

Mateo took a good, long look at Juan. "He doesn't look ready to me. He looks scared, and everyone knows if you show fear to the Devil, then the ground will open up and swallow you down, down, down! Into the very depths of hell itself!" Mateo laughed, truly enjoying himself.

Domingo whirled on Juan. "Are you scared?" he yelled. "Ah, tell me right now! Are you scared? Ah, what's wrong with you? Don't you love your mother? Don't you love your father? I'll thrash you good if you're scared, you stupid *cabezón!*"

Mateo appreciated Domingo's righteous anger, so he hit each of his brothers a couple of times, too. "You see, *burros,* what happens to you if you're not brave? You got to be brave at all times so that the Devil doesn't come in and steal your soul."

Both Alfonso and little Pelón lowered their heads and took their older brother's blows, just like Juan accepted Domingo's. After all, this was the way it was up here in the mountains of Jalisco. A boy had to endure much in order to become a proper Christian. As the good priest explained to them every time he came to their village, God's only Son, Jesus Christ, had come down upon the Earth to suffer for man's sins. So, the least a good Christian could do was to suffer along with Jesus in God's ongoing battle against the evil ways of *El Diablo.*

Just then, Emilia came running up. She was almost fifteen years old and older than all of them. "Stop hitting him!" she told Domingo. Emilia had reddish-brown hair just like Domingo and bright blue eyes like their father. She was tall and slender and very beautiful. Her skin was so white that it hurt her to spend much time in the sun.

"I thought I'd catch you out here bullying Juan again." She turned Juan around by the shoulders to face her. "You don't have to do this, you know. When the priest marries them, he is going to bless their wedding and so all this will be . . ."

"But the priest won't dare mention that Luis' mother is *una bruja!*" said Domingo, cutting her off. "You know very well that ever since the witch sent that basket of peaches and the fine fat chicken to the old priest in town, and he choked to death on that chicken bone, no one—but no one— dares to even bring up her name for fear of her putting a spell of death on them, too!"

"That's true," said Lucha. "You have to admit that, Emilia. This new young priest is never going to even mention her name." She made the sign of the cross over herself. "May the soul of the old priest rest in Heaven, dear God," she added.

Emilia looked from Domingo to Juan. Her eyes filled with tears as she took her little brother in her arms. "Oh, Juan, Juan, my little baby brother, Juan. I just don't know what to do. Maybe we should just go ask Mamá or Luisa. They always know what to do."

"No!" shouted Domingo. "That would be the worst thing we could do! Luisa can't possibly speak out against her future mother-in-law. And our mother—what can she do except tell us to pray? Or worse still, have us go talk with the priest, and we all know that he's deathly afraid of La Bruja. Remember, he's the one who heard the old priest's last words, 'Josefina, Josefina,' just before he . . ."

"Oh, my Lord God!" said Lucha. "You just said her name, Domingo!"

Instantly, Domingo dropped to his knees, quickly making the sign of the cross over himself and asking as fast as he could for God to protect him. Everyone else fell to their knees, too, crossing themselves and praying . . . except Juan, who remained on his feet.

"Eh, wait," said Juan, deep in thought. "Just how could the old priest's last words have been . . ." Everyone stared at him. He stopped himself. "I mean, when someone is choking on a chicken bone, they can't talk, can they? Every time I've almost choked, I couldn't talk. So how could the old priest have said La Bruja's name if he was choking to death, eh?"

"Are you questioning the good priest's word?" snapped Domingo, still on his knees.

"Well, no," said Juan, "I'm not. But I was only thinking that maybe . . ."

"Stop thinking!" exploded Domingo, getting to his feet. "You know very well that 'thinking' is one of the cardinal sins that caused our fall from the Garden of Eden!"

"Yes, I know," said Juan, "but I was only trying to say that . . ."

"Stop it, Juan!" demanded Domingo. "No more of this! It's time for you to stand up like a proper Christian and do what you have to do to save our family! Don't you love your mother? Eh, answer me! Don't you love our dear, beloved mother?"

"Well, yes, I do, of course," said Juan.

"And don't you love our father?"

Juan wanted to think about this one. At times he wasn't quite sure if he did. His father was always so mean to him, hitting him on the head and calling him 'cabezón.'

"Well, answer me!" ordered Domingo. "You love your father, don't you?"

Juan glanced up at his brother. At times like this, Domingo looked so much like their father that it was scary. His whole face was red with rage and his blue eyes were all glassed over, looking almost white.

"Yes," said Juan, not wanting to get hit anymore.

"Good," said Domingo, "then go do it right now!"

"But how are we to know if he really goes all the way to La Bruja's house and does it?" asked Mateo. "He could just go halfway across the valley and we'd never know. The way the moon is going in and out of those clouds, it's going to be hard to see him after he crosses that first fence."

"That's true," said Lucha, looking across the valley into the darkness. "After that first fence, we won't be able to see what he does if the moon goes behind the clouds."

"Oh, just leave him alone!" said Emilia, tears coming to her eyes once more. "It's enough that he's even attempting to do it! If you bigger ones are so doubtful, then why don't you just go along with him or, better still, do it yourself?"

"Well, no, we can't do that," said Lucha defensively. "We'd, ah, well, be sure to wake up her dogs because there'd be too many of us and then we'd all be killed."

Domingo shoved Lucha. "That was really a dumb thing

to say," he said. "We're trying to give him reassurance, not scare him." He turned to Juan. "Look, Juan, it's not her dogs that we're afraid of. Right, Mateo?"

"Yeah, sure, right," said Mateo.

"The reason that we don't go along with you, little brother, and protect you is that then you wouldn't have the chance to prove how brave you are. And, after all, that's the only thing that defeats the Devil . . . when a man is willing to meet El Diablo all by himself with nothing between him and eternal damnation but the faith he has in Almighty God."

"That's true!" said Mateo, making the sign of the cross over himself and kissing the back of his thumb, which was folded over his index finger in the form of the cross. "The only weapon a true Christian needs against all evil is the faith he carries here, inside of his chest! Oh, I envy you, Juan. When you succeed doing this tonight, not only will you be saving all your family, but you'll be saving the whole world, too. For, remember what the good priest says, 'One man's battle in overcoming the Devil's way is all mankind's salvation!' " Mateo smiled, feeling proud of how well he'd repeated the words of God that they'd learned in church.

Juan saw Mateo's straight white teeth smiling across his wide, handsome Indian face, and he felt a sudden strength come shooting up into his chest. Mateo was absolutely right. He just hadn't looked at it like that. This was, indeed, a chance for Juan to prove—not just to his family but to all the world—how much he loved them, just as Christ Himself had done on the cross. And so as long as he kept faith here inside his heart and soul, then no wrong could possibly come to him.

But before Juan could speak, telling them about his newly-found courage, Emilia spoke. "No! This is wrong! What if he fails?!" she said. "If you think this is so grand, Mateo, then why don't you and Domingo—who are so good with rocks—go do it. At least you'll have a chance if her killer dogs happen to wake up!"

Then, right then, was when it happened. It came up out of Juan before he even realized that he'd spoken. "No!" he said to Emilia, whom he knew truly loved him and only wanted the best for him. "I will not fail!" he shouted. "I will not fail! And the Earth will not open up and swallow me, for I love my mother, I truly do. And I will save us all. I don't want us burning in the fires of hell for all damnation!" His eyes began to cry, but his heart held strong. He turned and started for the creek.

Quickly, Pelón rushed after Juan. The two boys were friends. Over the years, their older brothers had forced them to fight each other many times, but their hearts had never really been in it. "Here," said Pelón, giving Juan his special rock. "I found this little rock inside the church one day. I think it came from Jesus' feet when they were repairing the walls."

"Gracias," said Juan, taking the well-worn, smooth little stone.

Pelón gave Juan a quick *abrazo* and then watched him go down the slope to the creek and hop from rock to rock so he wouldn't get wet.

"But how will we know if he goes all the way?" asked Mateo again.

"That's right," said Lucha. "How will we know?"

Domingo thought a moment, then shouted after Juan,

who was quickly disappearing into the night. "Bring back a peach!"

Juan just kept walking.

"Maybe he didn't hear you," said Lucha, so she screamed out, "Bring back a peach so we'll know you went all the way!"

"Quiet!" said Emilia. "What do you want to do? Wake up the dogs so they'll be sure to kill him?"

"But he didn't answer," said Lucha.

"He heard us," said Domingo, smiling. "No more shouting. Emilia is right. We don't want to wake up the dogs. My little brother needs a fair chance." He took a big breath. "Look at him go. He really is a brave little kid, isn't he?"

"Yes," said Pelón quietly, tears running down his wide cheeks. "Very, very brave."

*   *   *

" 'Bring back a peach!' they yell after me," said Juan in disgust to himself as he kept walking. "What do they think I am, one of the wise men to bring them Christmas presents? My God, the last person who tried to steal some peaches off her trees she hit on the head so hard with a club that it's said that the poor old man lost his memory and now thinks he belongs to her, and she works him like a slave from sun to sun.

"Oh, yes, I'll bring you back a peach—six of them wrapped in chocolate—so you'll see once and for all that I did it and our Mamá isn't going to have to burn in hell for all eternity."

Juan wiped the tears that came to his eyes and continued talking to himself as he walked across the valley, rubbing the little stone that Pelón had given him. "Oh, Lord God, why does it always have to happen to me? Ah? Why me? If I'm not getting hit for losing a goat to the coyote, then I'm getting hit because the pigs ate the chayote plant. Oh, I pray for the day that it isn't me that needs to get hit on the head, dear God.

"By the way," Juan continued, getting a twinkle in his eyes as he came to the first fence made of stone, "next week is Your Beloved Son's birthday, right?" He put his right hand on the rock fence and looked up at the heavens. The moon was smiling down on him between two great white clouds. "Well, then, Dear God, I'd like to dedicate what I'm about to do tonight as a Christmas gift to Your Most Beloved Son for His birthday. How about that? Pretty good, eh, dear God?"

And having said this, Juan laughed and climbed over the first rock fence on his way to the witch's house. He felt pretty good now. He liked the way he'd slipped this one in on God. After all, by offering to dedicate what he was about to do tonight to God's only Son, then God couldn't very well let him fail, could He? No, of course not. So now it was in the bag, because God had to make sure that he, Juan, succeeded so that His Most Beloved Son, Jesus Christ, wouldn't be disappointed on His birthday.

Feeling much better, Juan continued at a brisk pace across the valley. With God indebted to him, what could possibly go wrong? Nothing, absolutely nothing. The five big dogs would be sound asleep, and the biggest, juiciest peaches would be down on the lower branches so he could just pick them as easy as he pleased.

He stopped. He could now make out the individual peach trees by the side of La Bruja's house. He took a big breath. It was said that the reason her trees were so big and green and had the biggest, sweetest peaches in all the region was because she fed the trees the blood and guts of her chickens.

And once, long ago when Domingo and Mateo were little, they said that they'd actually witnessed her feeding her trees. It had just been dusk when Mateo and Domingo had sneaked up to her place to steal some of her fine peaches. She'd come out of her house, singing, with a big fat chicken under her arm. She was petting the chicken with such love when she'd suddenly taken a little knife from under her dress and slit the chicken's throat so quickly that they could hardly believe that she'd done it. Then she began to dance around her beloved trees, holding the big chicken upside down by its feet, singing with gusto as she fed the chicken's dripping blood to her trees. She raised the dead chicken to the sky, and they'd heard her summon the powers of the Devil to give her the greatest peaches. Domingo and Mateo had barely crawled away with their lives intact. She'd been as quick as lightning with that chicken-killing knife.

Remembering this story, Juan took a few deep breaths. "Oh, Dear God," he said, "remember, we got a deal. So no matter how quick she is with that knife of hers, You got to keep brave and stay by my side ready to help me out. Or, remember, Your Most Beloved Son might not find a present waiting for Him on His birthday, and then He'll be so, so sad. And you don't want to see Your Beloved Son all sad and red-eyed, do You? Of course, You don't. The poor Boy, His eyes are so red all the time, hanging on that cross. So let's be sure He gets a good birthday, ah, God?"

Having said this, Juan laughed and looked out across

the valley to the witch's house. He figured that it was best to keep working God as he went along. That way, God wouldn't get distracted with the other jobs that he had going across the universe, and He'd remember to keep Juan in mind.

He could now see that La Bruja's house wasn't very far. He'd have to keep his wits about him and make sure that her dogs weren't out hunting in the fields around her house. Because if he came upon her dogs out in the open fields, then they'd get him for sure. It was said that she had the meanest dogs in all the region, because she deliberately kept them half-starved.

It made Juan's skin want to crawl when he remembered what happened to that poor stranger who'd been caught by her dogs last year. He'd been riding this horse across the valley when he'd caught the scent of her wonderful-smelling peaches. So he'd reined in his horse and followed the scent. With his nose in the breeze, he'd ridden into her orchard thinking he'd found Heaven. But when he'd reached up to pick a big juicy peach, the dog called El Diablo had leaped out of nowhere, roaring like death itself as he'd caught the horse by the head. The other dogs bit at the horse's legs and flank and the horse went bucking, kicking through the orchard, falling over backwards.

The man was thrown off his horse and his pistol was ripped out of his hands before he could defend himself. The five big starving dogs started tearing at him and his horse in a frenzy of wild hunger. Kicking and whinnying, the horse was finally able to get to his feet and take off, but the man couldn't get up and kept screaming cries of agony until the witch came out of her house, calling off her dogs.

Getting to the second stone wall, Juan stopped to catch

his breath. Her house was right ahead of him now, and her orchard of peach trees started just on the other side of that last rock wall. He glanced up at the full moon and then back across the valley to where he'd left Domingo and the others. But he couldn't see them anymore. In fact, he could barely make out the dark outline of the pig pens and the horse corrals behind them. He could see his parents' house easily. The bright light from the kitchen could be seen through the window. He wondered if he couldn't just turn around now and go back home. After all, to have come this far in the dark, he'd already shown the Devil that he was pretty darn brave.

"Look, God," he said out loud, "people ride their horses clear around this side of the valley so they don't have to come near her orchard. I've already come closer to her place in the night than few mortals would dare. So what do You think, eh, God? Do I really have to go any further? The Devil can already see that I'm pretty brave."

Suddenly, the moon went behind some dark clouds and the night darkened and turned cold. Instantly, Juan's eyes got big.

"All right, all right, God!" he said quickly. "I'll go all the way. Just don't take my moonlight away. I need all the light I can get."

The moon came out from behind the clouds and the night was bright with light once more.

He took a big breath and made the sign of the cross over himself, kissing the back of his thumb, which was folded over his index finger in the form of a cross, just like he'd seen Mateo do. He blew out and continued across the open field toward the witch's home—this woman, this person who grew the finest peaches in all the region.

Suddenly, Juan thought he heard something and he stopped dead. Slowly, carefully, he glanced around, hoping to God that it wasn't her dogs that had sneaked up on him. But he saw nothing. And the moon was now out from between the clouds, and it was so huge and bright and big around that it illuminated the whole area around him almost as bright as day. He could see her house clearly, too. Why, he could actually begin to make out the individual stones of the rock fence around her home.

Then, as he was studying her place carefully, he spotted the huge dog. His heart stopped. Good God, it was the famous dog, El Diablo, and there he was up on her porch, stretching and yawning with his open mouth so gigantic— reaching up toward the moon—that Juan was sure that his whole leg could fit inside.

Juan swallowed, not moving a muscle. The huge dog continued yawning and stretching. If the monster dog El Diablo was up and about, then Juan figured that her other four dogs were up and about, too. Without moving his head, Juan quickly rolled his eyes about, carefully searching for the other dogs around the house. For Juan well knew that the most dangerous dog for him this night wasn't El Diablo, her biggest dog, but Cara Chata, her smallest dog. For in this area of Mexico, every ranch kept a pack of dogs, and among their pack they always had a nervous little dog that was a light sleeper so it would start barking at the slightest sound and wake up the larger dogs.

Juan searched her porch with his eyes, examining every potted plant, then carefully looked around her famous mango tree. It was said that mango trees couldn't live up in this mountainous region of Jalisco, Mexico, that mangoes were strictly tropical fruit trees, so they could only grow big and strong and bear fruit further south in the regions of Guerrero and Oaxaca. And yet, there stood Josefina's mango tree alongside her house, as big and as strong as a fully-grown oak and full of fruit as huge around as bull's . . .

Juan stopped his thoughts. "Good God," he said to himself. "I just thought of her name inside my head! I wonder if she also knows when people think about her?" Just then, as he had this thought, the door flew open with a bang and out came the witch herself. She was a tall, well-built woman with big, strong hands and large calloused feet. It was said that she always worked barefooted and she was never without a shovel or hoe in her hand. She'd always done all her own work—building fences, planting trees, hauling dirt—until she'd hit that poor old man on the head a few years back. And now she had him working with her from sun to sun.

"*¡Perrrros!*" she said to the dogs. "Here are a few scraps, but I'm not feeding you too much tonight."

Quickly, all the dogs got to their feet and she threw them the scraps. Juan crouched down into a little ball, holding as still as he could. He was out in midfield with nothing between him and the terrible witch. The rock fence that he'd just climbed over was quite a ways behind him.

"Oh, dear God," he prayed, "please don't let her see me."

"I want all of you dogs staying alert tonight," she said, petting her pack of hungry beasts. "It's a full moon, a good night for some no-good, lazy so-and-so to try and steal some fruit off my trees. So you keep alert or I'll cut your guts out and feed them to my trees, too!

"Here, Diablito," she said to her huge black dog, calling him Little Devil, "you be extra ready tonight. I got this strange feeling that something very, very strange is going to happen tonight." Then she suddenly turned and looked straight out at Juan. "What is that funny little clump I see out in my field? Ah, answer me! Are you a rock that fell off my stone fence, or what?"

Juan squeezed his eyes closed, hoping he could just disappear. "Dear Lord God," he said to himself, "what are You doing? I thought we had a deal! Oh, please, dear God, help me! Help me! I'm just a little boy!"

"Oh, so you won't answer me!" yelled the witch at the clump that she thought might be a rock. "All right, then, take this!" And she picked up a stone from the pile of rocks she kept on her porch and threw it with all her strength at the clump, almost hitting Juan. "I can see you, you no-good thief! Don't you dare think I can't see in the dark! The full moon is my friend, and you come any closer to my winter peaches and I'll have my dogs on you in a second! Do you hear me? IN A SECOND!!" And then she lifted her mighty arms and screamed up toward the Heavens. "The full moon is my friend! And the old woman who lives up there looks out after me and my trees! Because we're both women! Do you hear me? Because we're both women all alone in the night! And we have our special ways!"

Juan didn't dare move a muscle. He was rolled up in a little ball, rooted to the ground. His eyes wouldn't even open. They were transfixed, staring into the eternal darkness of his own forgotten soul. Then he heard her door close with another big bang, and he figured she'd gone back inside. He could hear her dogs gnawing at their bones and lapping up the scraps. He figured that this was maybe his last chance to escape with his life. But he didn't dare get up and run, so he began to crawl backwards as fast as he could.

Just then the little dog called Cara Chata began barking.

"Oh, dear God," said Juan, "she's spotted me. I don't have a chance now. Good God, I was a fool to have let them talk me into doing this."

Then Juan heard the roar, the huge howling ROAR of El Diablo, and here came the pack of dogs flying off the porch straight toward him.

"Oh, dear God!" said Juan, almost peeing in his pants. "Now what am I to do? If I stay here, I'm sure to be ripped to pieces and eaten alive. But if I get up to run, they're sure to catch me, or . . . wait, what if I can make it to her peach trees over there and climb up a tree? Yes, that's it!" he said excitedly.

Juan tried to get to his feet so he could run as fast as he could to her peach trees, but he couldn't get up. Something was holding him down to the ground like a gigantic magnet. The pack of howling dogs was getting closer and closer, bellowing sounds of hell as they came, but Juan just couldn't get to his feet no matter how much he pushed against the Earth, trying to right himself so he could take off running. Carefully, he placed both of his hands against the ground in front of him and he pushed and pushed with all his might. But for the life of him, he just couldn't move himself even one inch. A gigantic hand-like force was holding him down tight to the Mother Earth.

Finally, he gave up. And in that instant when he gave up

and relaxed, he saw it. A female coyote was over there not far from him, sniffing in his direction. He looked at the coyote and she looked at him, and their eyes held on to each other for a long, long, heart-in-your-throat, timeless moment. Then the coyote smiled—actually smiled—at him, glanced at the pack of howling dogs, gave a yelping howl, and leaped over the rock fence, passing over the moon as graceful as a dream.

Juan couldn't believe what his eyes had just seen: a smiling female coyote leaping over the full moon. And so he relaxed, feeling the warmth of the gigantic hand that was holding him down against the rich, good-smelling earth. Suddenly he felt much better; he was safe now. All he had to do was stay still and the dogs would follow the coyote.

The pack of dogs came racing up, hollering as they came. Juan watched each one of them jump up on the fence, gather their feet under themselves and leap past the full moon, too. But not nearly as gracefully as the she-coyote had done.

Then all the big dogs were gone, giving chase to the coyote. Juan now thought that he was perfectly safe . . . until he realized that Cara Chata was staring at him, eyeball-to-eyeball. The little dog hadn't been able to make it over the fence, and her long tongue was hanging out as she now tried to catch her breath. Juan swallowed, not moving a muscle. "Oh, dear God," he said to himself, "I've been caught dead."

*   *   *

Back across the valley, Domingo and the others heard La Bruja's door open with a bang and then they heard her shout into the night.

"Do you think she saw him?" asked Emilia. "Oh, Lord God, we should never have allowed him to go!"

"Quiet!" said Domingo. "Let us hear!"

They heard another shout, even louder than the first, and then the door slammed shut.

"What do you think, Mateo?" asked Domingo. "Did she spot him?"

"No, I don't think so," said Mateo, "or we'd hear her dogs."

They listened to the silence of the night, wondering what was happening to Juan. Then suddenly they heard the high-pitched barking of the witch's little dog, and then came that huge, devastating ROAR of El Diablo, filling the whole valley with sound.

"Oh, good God!" yelled Emilia. "They're killing Juanito! Quick, let's go tell Mamá!"

"No!" said Domingo. "Do you want us all to get in trouble?"

"Besides," added Mateo, "they don't have him yet. Those barks are of dogs giving chase, not of dogs ripping and killing."

"That's true," said Lucha. "Dogs sound very different when they got their prey down on the ground. They're just chasing right now. Listen to them; our little brother must be really running," she said, smiling proudly. "He really went all the way. Wow, I wouldn't have ever REALLY gone all the way. Would you, Domingo?"

"Quiet!" he said. "We need to hear! Those dogs are going crazy! Just listen to them. He must be in the orchard, climbing a tree or something.

"See, Mateo," continued Domingo, turning to his friend.

"All these years I've been telling you that my little brother is brave. You're going to have to push Alfonso and Pelón a long way for them to match my little brother."

"We'll see, we'll see," said Mateo. "How do we know that the dogs aren't just chasing a coyote or something? For all we know, your brother could just be laying down by some rocks, hiding."

An adult voice suddenly startled them all. "What's going on?" asked José Villaseñor, coming up behind them. All six kids turned around and came face to face with José. And beside José stood Luis, as tall and wide as a giant.

"Eh?" continued José, glancing them over. "Why are those dogs barking? What mischief have you kids come to do behind the pig's pen? Come on, answer me. Mamá sent us down here, thinking you might be up to something."

His voice was calm. He always spoke very calmly. "Domingo," he said, "hear me good. Don't glance like that at Emilia again, or I'll take you down to size in front of everyone. Now talk. Quickly. What's going on?"

Mateo didn't dare do anything, either. The giant Luis had come in close to him and was ready to snatch him up by the throat if he so much as breathed. They were trapped. There was no getting around it, and Emilia was dying to talk.

"José," said Emilia, "they sent Juan to La Bruj—I mean to Don Luis' mother's house, and I told them not to, but Domingo kept insisting that . . ."

"Oh, no!" said Luis.

But José never said a word. He'd already turned and was racing toward the horse corrals. In a matter of seconds, he caught a horse, jumped on it bareback, and was racing off at a full gallop, leaping across the little creek.

Luis got a horse, too, and took off after José. Domingo and the other kids watched as both men disappeared into the night, horses' hooves pounding the good Earth with sound. The dogs continued howling in the distance, filling the night with terrible sound.

*   *   *

The short little dog called Cara Chata caught her breath and started barking into Juan's face, calling the pack of howling dogs back.

"Oh, my God!" said Juan to himself. He leaped to his feet. "I'll run to La Bruja's house and summon the Devil. Then I'll race to her orchard, pick a bunch of peaches, and take off back across the valley before her dogs return!"

Thinking that he had it easy now, Juan laughed at the barking little dog and dodged left, then right, then leaped over the short-legged little dog and took off racing toward the witch's house. But he hadn't gone more than ten feet before the stout little dog caught him by his leg, dragging him to the ground.

"You fool!" screamed Juan, kicking at her. "Don't you know I'm about God's business?!" But the little dog didn't seem to care, and she kept hold of Juan, growling and biting and snapping.

Juan finally broke loose and took off running with Cara Chata in fast pursuit, grabbing him and knocking him down every few feet.

"Now, what are You doing, God? Having fun? Well, it's

not funny to get past a pack of killer dogs only to have my feet chewed off by this little nothing-dog!"

Then Juan heard laughter, a great ROAR of huge laughter. He glanced up at the moon, thinking that God was now openly laughing at him. But then he realized that the laughter came from behind him. He turned, and there was the witch herself no more than twenty feet away. And she had a shovel in her hand, holding it like a club to do him in. His heart leaped into his throat.

"What have we here? A baby thief?" she yelled viciously.

Juan swallowed. "No!" he yelled, leaping to his feet and standing up as tall as he could. "I'm here to . . . to summon the Devil and all the forces of evil that you have in your great powers, and . . . and say that I don't fear you, or your witchcraft, for our familia walks in the love of Almighty God!

"DO YOU HEAR ME?" Juan added with all the power of his little seven-year-old heart and soul. "We do not fear you, for WE FOLLOW GOD'S PATH OF LOVE!!"

The large woman stopped dead in her tracks, not expecting this—especially not from such a small child. The little female dog, Cara Chata, also stopped yapping at Juan and stood there in the moonlight with her head cocked at an odd angle, looking at him in a strange way, too.

Juan made the sign of the cross over himself, kissed the back of his thumb that was folded over his index finger in the form of a cross and said, "The Earth shall not swallow me, and no harm shall ever come to my mother and my family, for I can truly say to you that I carry God's love here inside my heart and soul, and you are powerless before me."

Hearing these last words, La Bruja came out of her momentary surprise and said, "Powerless, am I? You little piece of chicken caca! We'll see! We'll see!" And she charged Juan, swinging at him with her shovel.

But from so many years of getting hit on the head, Juan was pretty agile. So he ducked her blows and took off running toward her orchard, heart pounding so fast that he was sure that it was going to come up his throat and jump out of his mouth. He swallowed again and again, trying to keep his pounding heart down in his chest as he ran. But here came Cara Chata again, trying to grab his legs. Juan jumped and jumped, hopped and hopped, dodged and kicked, and managed to keep going until he got to her peach trees.

Quickly, he glanced around for some fruit, but none was hanging from the lower branches; all the peaches were up high in the trees. It was strange, nobody in all the region had winter peaches except La Bruja. Juan was just deciding which tree to climb when he heard that huge, devastating roar of El Diablo. The pack of dogs was headed back his way.

Instantly, Juan climbed the tree nearest him as fast as a squirrel and picked one, two, three, four, five, six big peaches, swung down from the tree, gathered up his fruit and put it in his pouch, then took off racing as fast as he could. But the pack of dogs was on his tail. The witch, too.

"Good, God!" said Juan to himself as he ran, "I did it, God! I really did it! Even right to her face! So please don't let her killer dogs get me now!" He was racing across the open field as fast as he could go, hoping to get to the first rock fence, scramble over it, and then . . . oh, he just didn't know what to do. The big woman was going crazy, yelling at her dogs to hurry up and get the boy. "He's a thief! A thief!

Get him, Diablo! Get him and tear his no-good heart from his chest and eat it for your DINNER!!"

The moon was going in and out of clouds, giving the whole valley an eerie feeling. Juan got to the first fence and climbed up on top of it so he could look around. There came the pack of dogs, no more than a hundred yards away, hollering to the Heavens as they closed in on him. Right behind him came the witch, no more than fifty feet away.

Juan quickly glanced around and spotted a pile of big rocks not far out in the next field. "If I can get to those rocks, I'll have a fighting chance," he said. "But I'll need a club to fight the dogs off with. Oh, God, please help me!" he said, glancing up to the heavens.

Just then, as he asked for help, he saw the witch stop thirty feet away from him and raise the shovel above her head, whirling it around like a lariat. She sent it flying at him with all the power of her body, the whole while screaming, "May you burn in hell, you little no-good thief!"

Calmly, carefully, Juan watched the shovel coming right at him, long wooden handle following large spoon-like metal in a spinning circle of air-swishing noise. Smiling, Juan ducked, jumping off the rock fence, and the shovel passed right over him like a great ocean-sailing vessel.

"Gracias!" yelled Juan to the old witch, and he ran over and picked up the shovel and took off for the pile of big boulders out in midfield.

"Don't give me *'gracias'*!" screamed La Bruja, getting to the fence. "May your thieving soul burn in hell for all eternity! I've worked hard for what I got! Do you hear me?!" She kept yelling after Juan as she stood there by the fence she'd built with her own two hands. "I worked hard! And you have no right to enjoy the fruits of my labor! May you choke on the seed of my peaches! Choke! Choke! Choke! TO DEATH!!"

Hearing the words "Choke! Choke! Choke! TO DEATH!" as he ran, Juan thought it had been pretty stupid of him to have stolen so many peaches, because how could they really enjoy eating them, realizing that they came from the witch's trees and that an old priest had, indeed, choked to death while eating one of her fat chickens? He dropped the peaches. The big rocks were getting closer and closer as he ran, but her dogs were almost on top of him.

"Oh, dear God," said Juan, leaping over the grass and rough terrain as he went. "I did do wrong to steal her peaches because she does work hard to grow them. I see that now; I really do. So, could You please forgive me for my trespasses, like I forgive others for their trespasses? And from now on, I'm the biggest forgiver of trespasses You've ever seen! No kidding, dear God! The biggest!"

He could hear the dogs getting closer and closer. He turned and saw that the huge black dog was leading the pack. They were no more than thirty yards away from him, howling to the heavens with vengeance. "Oh, MAMÁ! MAMÁ! Help me!" yelled Juan. "I think God has forgotten me!"

He pumped his little legs as hard as he could, trying to get to the boulders before the pack overtook him. He figured that if he could just get to the rocks and scramble up, then he could maybe fight them off with the shovel. The rocks were getting bigger and bigger as his little legs went flying.

"You won't make it to those rocks!" the witch yelled at him. "And if you do, my dog El Diablo will pull you off of them and eat you alive!"

She began to laugh and shout and sing. "Ha, ha, ha! You're going to get yours! Ha, ha, ha! All of you thieving men are going to get yours. This is judgment day FOR ALL OF YOU!"

"Boy, she's not very forgiving of other's trespasses," said Juan to himself as he ran. "I wonder if she's dancing, too?"

He was tempted to turn around and take a quick look at her, but he knew he couldn't. The dogs were almost on top of him. He could feel their breathing, and they smelled awful.

Then he reached the big rocks and was just scrambling up when he felt a sharp, tearing pain in his left foot as he was being dragged down off the rocks. He turned and saw that El Diablo had him by the foot and was trying to get his whole leg into his huge mouth, growling and biting and yanking and ripping. Juan kicked and jerked and SCREAMED at the top of his lungs, and tried hitting the monstrous dog with the shovel. But then the other dogs came, leaping on him from all sides, ready to devour him, too.

The last thing Juan saw before he passed out was the form of a huge horse-like creature with wings come flying out of the Heavens, smashing into the pack of dogs. Then a mighty angel was swinging a club with a head of steel, lashing dogs left and right, cutting them to pieces as they yelped in pain. Then a larger angel also appeared, and this angel grabbed El Diablo by the throat, strangling him.

All this time, La Bruja was weeping hysterically, and yelling, "No, no, no! Please, no, no, no!" The larger angel turned and took La Bruja into his arms with such tenderness, calling her "Mamá." Juan thought that was so, so, so funny. He'd never for the life of him thought that witches could also be loving mothers, especially not of angels. And that was the last thing Juan remembered. Then he was gone, done, no more.

*   *   *

Waking up, Juan found that he was in bed under the covers in his parents' bedroom. His whole body was in pain. Why, it hurt his head to just move his eyes to look around the room. He tried to lick his lips, but his mouth was so dry that he had trouble moving his tongue. He swallowed a few times. He was so thirsty that he didn't know what to do. Water. He needed lots of water, right now. He tried to get up to go get some water, but when he moved, his whole body screamed out in terrible pain.

"Oh, my God!" he said. "What happened to me?"

"Mamá, he's woken up," Juan heard Emilia yell in the distance.

"About time!" Juan heard his mother answer from another room. "It's been nearly three days!" Then he heard his mother's feet come rushing over the tile floor, with sister Emilia right behind her.

"So, you've finally come back from the dead," said his mother, smiling at him. "Oh, *mi hijito,* you gave us an awful scare. But what ever possessed you to do such a crazy thing? You know very well how Domingo and those wild boys are about everything. Did you really think that their interpretation of God's wishes would be any different than what they think of the rest of the world?" Gently, she took the back of his head with her right hand and lifted him up just a little so she could spoon-feed the watery fluid that she'd prepared for him.

"Oh, *mi hijito,* I'm so surprised at you. You're my last-born son, and all these years I've been raising you to realize down deep inside yourself that the things of men aren't necessarily true. Especially not when they hurt you or cause harm to others."

Juan heard his mother's words as in a far-away dream, and he felt the warm, watery liquid go slowly down his throat. Then he was sound asleep once more, dreaming, dreaming, seeing that flying horse and angel come swooping down out of the Heavens and once more scattering the pack of mad dogs. The female coyote came to him again, and she smiled. Juan felt so warm and good all over with the female coyote at his side. Then his head was being raised up again and he was spoon-fed some more warm, watery liquid. When he opened his eyes, he saw that his mother was, indeed, the female coyote and she was smiling down on him as she fed him. Now he realized why that female coyote had been so willing to lead the pack of dogs away from him. Why, the female coyote had been his own beloved mother.

"Drink up," his mother was now saying as she fed him with the smooth-feeling wooden spoon. "And keep in mind as you grow stronger that, all these years, I've been raising you to be a gentle man—not a lost male who destroys all he lays his hands on because he feels so left out of the joy of giving birth.

"Oh, *mi hijito,* I love you, I love you so much. And you must promise me to never do such a thing without consulting me first. You've become a little man, *mi hijito,* and a man always needs a woman's opinion in order to round out his decisions—like the broken rocks need the river waters to smooth out their rough edges and make the rocks smooth and round and whole. Believe me, no man's decisions are complete without a woman's influence. And no woman's garden can give life without a man's participation.

"Which leads me to another point, *mi hijito*. I want you to realize that Doña Josefina is no witch. I don't care what all the people say about her. She isn't a *bruja*. She's just a lonely, bitter woman who has tilled her garden alone all these years, because she was wronged by a man in her youth—as so many women have been wronged by men since the beginning of time. And so she has strange ways and doesn't trust any man, especially not since that old mule driver abused her, too. But she's basically a good woman, *mi hijito*—a little crazy and scared like so many of us when we lose our faith in God. But, believe me, she's no witch. That's just the rumor that people like to pass around, especially men who can't stand to see a woman doing well all on her own.

"Here, drink up. We've got to get you strong again. Christmas is only a few days away, and then a week later we have the wedding. That poor woman, she works so hard for her peaches and she'd have none to sell if she didn't have you boys intimidated by her wild ways."

As he sipped the liquid from the smooth-feeling spoon, Juan could see that his mother really liked this woman who'd he'd always known as a witch. He could also see that, yes, indeed, his mother was a coyote. She really was. Her eyes, her mouth, her kind loving touch. She was absolutely a wonderful, loving female-coyote, and she'd been the one who'd come to his rescue when the pack of dogs had been upon him.

Then Juan heard heavy footsteps, and into the room came José and Luis.

"Juan," said José. "Luis is here to see you. He's been coming to see you every day since the accident."

"That was no accident," said Luis with power. "That was a message sent to Luisa and me straight from God! Now we can go into our marriage with open hearts! Juanito, you saved the day for us by bringing everything out into the open that everyone has been talking about for years all over the valley, but has never had the guts to come and say to my face or to my beloved mother's face!"

"Are you two the ones, the . . . the angels who got the dogs off me?" asked Juan, not quite able to fully see yet.

José grinned. "Yes, Luis and I are those angels."

Luis came close and took Juan's hand gently. "We destroyed all the dogs. Now you can come by our home without fear any time you please. I swear, *en el otro mundo no hay mal, pero en este mundo ¿quién sabe con todo los miedos y celos que la gente esconde en sus corazones?*" In the other world there is no evil, Luis had said, but in this world, who can know with all the fears and jealousy that people hide in their hearts?

"You are *mi amo*," continued Luis, "you are my soul, my hero, my savior. And my poor mother will come around to saying the same thing once she gets over mourning for her dogs. Yes, we had to kill them all, except for Cara Chata. She wasn't biting you when we ran up. No, like the proper little lady she is, she'd figured that she'd done her job of calling in the pack, and so she was just sitting back and watching with that head of hers tilted at that funny little angle she always gets." Luis laughed. "You are *mi amo*, my hero, and I give you homage!" Then he kissed Juan on the forehead ever so gently.

"All right, no more now," siad Doña Margarita. "That's enough for today. He needs to sleep so he can regain his strength. Oh, I knew those wild boys were up to no good when I sent you two to go check on them. I could feel it in my bones."

"And you were right, Mamá," said José. "We just barely got there in time."

"Yes," said Luis, "and if José wasn't the greatest horseman in all the region, he wouldn't have been able to clear those rock fences with such ease riding bareback and get there before the dogs did even more damage."

Juan heard no more. He was off in dream once again and the smiling coyote was by his side, keeping watch over him. He smiled back at the coyote, feeling so happy, and Luis' words *"en el otro mundo no hay mal,"* continued singing in his brain. Then he realized that yes, indeed, his own beloved mother could turn herself into a she-coyote at will, but this didn't make her a witch, either. No, she was simply a powerful woman who was wild of heart. There were no witches. There was no evil on the other side. That was all just a rumor coming out of the fear and jealousy that people hide in their hearts.

*   *   *

It was Christmas day. The whole house smelled of cooking and baking, and there was much activity in the front of the house. All the family was present: thirty-some cousins and their fathers and mothers. Don Pío, Juan's grandfather on his mother's side, had also come up the mountain from the town of Piedra Gorda, Fat Rock, with his young bride.

Emilia and José came into the bedroom where Juan was staying. Emilia said, "Come on, lazy bones! Mamá has said to bring you into the living room where we've set up a special chair for you!" She was so happy. It made Juan feel all warm inside.

José picked up Juan in his arms, being careful not to touch the leg that El Diablo had almost eaten, and carried him across the house. All the children came rushing to Juan. He was the talk of the whole valley. In fact, it was now said that Juan was a boy so brave that the blood ran backwards from his heart.

Domingo watched all the cousins give Juan greeting and ask him if it was true that he'd faced the witch eye-to-eye in midfield and had single-handedly fought her pack of dogs to a standstill. Seeing all the cousins speak to Juan with such adoration, Domingo's face filled with rage and jealousy.

Suddenly, out of nowhere, Domingo felt a powerful hand grip his shoulder. It was José. "If you want people to look at you like that, little brother," José said, "then next time you do your own dirty work and don't push people littler than you to do it for you."

"But he's the youngest!" snapped Domingo. "The purest of heart! And the priest has always told us that . . ."

"Don't give me that," said José calmly. "We both know that you can always take the words of the Bible or the words of the priest and twist them into any sneaky act you want to do. Remember what our beloved mother always adds to the Bible or the priest's words: Does it harm anyone? Does it cause more pain and darkness? Or does it bring a little more peace and understanding among all of us lost mortals?

"Look at me in the eyes. You're no fool, Domingo. You're smart and could be a good leader, but—and I say this with all sincerity—you've got to stop sneaking off behind pig pens to do your glorious deeds." Eye-to-eye, both brothers held. One was small and dark and older. The other was fair-headed, large-boned and younger.

The tension was so great that Domingo was ready to explode. But just then the front door opened, and in came Luis with his mother. The woman was all dressed up and had a basket covered with a cloth in her hand. In all these years, no one had ever seen La Bruja dressed up like a lady. The room went silent. Even Don Juan, the children's father, who'd been talking loudly and drinking tequila with a couple of his fair-skinned relatives, stopped his words. No one moved. Everyone stared in complete silence—adults and children alike. It was Doña Margarita, who had been talking to Don Pío and his beautiful young bride, who finally got up and went across the room. She walked right up to the tall, handsome woman and her son, who both towered over her.

"Welcome to our humble home, Doña Josefina," said Doña Margarita. "This is, indeed, a glorious day for us to finally have you here with us under our roof. Merry Christmas!"

"Merry Christmas," said the tall, powerful woman. Cautiously, she glanced around the room at the dozens and dozens of faces that she'd seen at a distance over the years, but never up this close. "The honor is mine, Doña Margarita. I feel . . . well, most happy that you've invited me and my son to spend this most holy day of Jesus Christ's birthday with you and your family."

Some people were heard to inhale sharply, being taken aback by the fact that the witch had dared pass God's Most Sacred Son's name through her lips.

But Doña Margarita wasn't surprised at all, and said, "From now on, you and your son will always be invited to pass the holy days of Christmas with us. For let it be known," she added, taking La Bruja by the hand and turning to everyone in the room, "that from now on, Doña Josefina and her son Luis are part of *nuestra familia* and they are both to be loved and respected as our family members here on Earth and afterwards in Heaven, too!"

A couple of the younger cousins giggled. "Here on Earth, maybe yes," one whispered, "but how is a witch supposed to ever get into Heaven?" All the kids giggled.

Juan's mother turned toward Juan and the children, saw them giggling, and came flying toward them, bringing the witch with her by the hand. "And, children, I want you each to meet Doña Josefina personally and shake hands with her."

The kids froze in terror. Domingo and a few others quickly tried to crouch down and sneak away, but there was José on one side of them, and here came Luis on the other side. Domingo froze, and so did the others who'd been thinking of getting away.

"Come on, step forward one at a time and shake hands with Doña Josefina," said Doña Margarita once again. But no child would dare come forward. They all held back in dreaded terror. They didn't care what Doña Margarita said;

they knew that this woman was evil to the bottom of her heart.

Seeing how terrified the children were of her, Doña Josefina took a big breath and then said, "They don't have to shake my hand, Doña Margarita." Tears came to her eyes. "Children, after all, really do no more . . . than what their parents would truly like to do themselves, but . . . don't have the guts . . . to come forward and do it!"

A hush of whispers went through the room.

Wiping her eyes, Doña Josefina turned to her son Luis. "Come, let's go. I'd told you it was a mistake for you to bring me here today. These fine people will never accept me in a million years!"

"But Mamá," said Luis helplessly, "we've got to try and . . ."

"Then stay if you like!" she snapped. "But I'm leaving!" And she turned with all the dignity she could muster and started to go when a voice behind her said, "I'd like to shake your hand, señora."

It was a child's voice, and La Bruja stopped dead in her tracks. She and everyone else turned to see who had spoken. The group of children opened up, and there sat Juan in the big chair that had been prepared for him. He swallowed, then repeated himself. "I'd like to shake your hand, señora."

"Eh, aren't you the one who . . ." the big woman stopped her words. Juan's hands and arms and legs were still all covered with swollen bruises and large reddish-black wounds.

"Yes," said Juan, "I'm the one and, well, I want to say that I'm sorry for . . . for . . ." Tears came to his eyes and he had to swallow several times before he could go on. The room was silent. "I mean, I know you work real hard to grow your peaches, señora, and I had no right to steal them, even if I think you are a witch."

People gasped. Others choked. The whole room was filled with a nervous hush of coughing and breathing. Some people began to fan themselves, trying to get air.

"Juan, you must apologize for what you said," said Doña Margarita.

"No, señora," said Doña Josefina, "please don't have him apologize for simply saying what he really thinks. For the truth is that half of the good people in this room think the same thing but do not have the nerve to say it to my face." She glanced around the room, looking from face to face. The room was absolutely still. Then she turned back to Juan. "Thank you, child, for acknowledging that I do work hard to grow my peaches. I accept your apology. And about your thinking I'm a witch, well, what can I say, except that . . ."

"You don't have to explain yourself, Mamá!" bellowed Luis, standing up tall, the cords of his powerful neck coming up like ropes, he was so mad.

"But I want to explain," said his mother. "I don't want you having to run away from this valley like your brother had to do."

She took a deep breath. "I'm no witch," she said to everyone—men, women and children. "Do you hear me? I'm no bruja. Yes, maybe I've acted like one over the years, being over-protective of my trees. And using manure and animals' guts and blood to feed my trees has, I'm sure, caused much talk, too, but . . . but that doesn't make me a witch! That just makes me a woman who doesn't have much trust in people—especially men—and shows that I know what I'm doing when it comes to growing plants and trees.

"My mango tree, my winter peaches, they aren't the accomplishments of witchcraft. No, they are the accomplishments of, well . . ." Tears came to her eyes. ". . . of science, which the old priest in town taught me along with so many other wonders of life." She stopped her words and began to cry. Luis took his mother in his arms, holding her tenderly. Luisa also came up and hugged her mother-in-law-to-be.

A few people began to whisper, but no one spoke aloud. They were stunned. They were shocked. They'd never expected in a hundred million years to see this big, powerful, wild woman—whom they'd all considered to be a witch—to be crying like this, so tenderly, on her son's massive shoulder.

"All right," said Doña Margarita, stepping forward after a proper quiet moment. "As I was saying, I want each of the children to meet you, Doña Josefina, and Juan here has volunteered to be the first."

"Oh, yes, excuse me," said the large woman, "just let me dry my eyes, please."

And so everyone watched as this powerful woman dried her eyes and then stepped forward to meet little Juan. "I'm so glad to meet you," she said, smiling. "In the last few days, my son Luis has told me so much about you."

She reached out, giving Juan her huge, hard hand. Juan looked at the big fingers and calloused palm and then took it. It felt as heavy as a large stone.

"Merry Christmas," she said, eyes full of merriment. "And look, I've brought you a basket of peaches." They were the largest, prettiest peaches anyone had ever seen. "And from now on," she continued saying to Juan, "whenever you want some, just come by the house and we'll pick them together. That way, you won't get green ones like you did the other night."

"Those were green?" asked Juan, astonished.

"Yes," she said, laughing. "Green-green!"

"Oh, no!" said Juan, laughing, too. Then, looking at the basket full of peaches and smelling the rich aroma, Juan took one and bit into it. "Oh, my God, this is heaven!" he said.

"Exactly!" said the tall woman. "And those were the exact same words the poor old priest always used to tell me, too," she said, tears coming to her eyes again. "Oh, he was a good man, a very good man, God rest his soul in heaven," she added, making the sign of the cross over herself. "I loved him; I truly loved him. He was my everything good and bad here on Earth, all wrapped up in one blessed human being, so help me God!"

And in that instant, all the people in the room realized who José-Luis' father was. Why, this large, tall woman and the old priest had loved each other as a man and a woman.

Quickly, others started making the sign of the cross over themselves, too. For this was, indeed, a special moment, a holy moment. God had come down upon the Earth and visited them, His people, in all His power and mystery and miraculous wonders of love.

Then a child spoke—the smallest child in the room who could speak. "If I shake your hand and let you hug me and kiss me," said the child, "will you give me a peach, too?"

People started laughing, melting, relaxing.

"Why, yes," said Doña Josefina, "certainly."

"Oh, good, Señora Witch!" shouted the little girl, throwing open her tiny arms for a big hug and kiss.

The whole room exploded with laughter. Even Domingo was finally caught up in the whole spirit of the moment.

So the child and Josefina hugged each other, and the rest of the day went beautifully. People were so filled with happiness that they just couldn't stop from smiling and laughing as they ate all the special foods and drank all the special drinks that had been prepared all week long. The much-feared woman of their valley wasn't a witch, after all. No, she was just a poor lost soul, like each one of them when they were alone and scared.

Juan sat there on his throne-like chair like a little king, rejoicing in God's Only Beloved Son's birthday. And when the time came to sing to Jesus for His birthday, Juan would swear that he actually saw Jesus stop looking so sad hanging there on the cross over the doorway. And He straightened up and cast a big smile at Juan, winking His left eye.

*   *   *

Author's Note

My father always explained to me the story that made him into the man that he later became. "When you bully people and lie and cheat, you do it because you're scared," he told me, "and you become a small, frightened person. But when you stand up to the truth with all your love and heart and soul, no matter what, you become brave and strong and develop guts!"

Remembering my father's words, years later when a large picture window was broken at our home, I called my boys and their ten cousins together and asked who did it. No one would talk. I demanded for them to have the guts to be truthful. One little cousin finally spoke up and said that he'd thrown the rock, but that my son had ducked and so that's why the window was broken.

"So are you saying that my son broke it because he ducked?"

"Well, yes, in a way."

"Look," I said, "stop passing the buck. You're not a politician. Have some guts and tell me who's responsible."

He was scared. Really scared. But finally he said, "I did it. I broke the window."

"Great," I said, and I pulled out a twenty-dollar bill and gave it to him. He was shocked and now everyone wanted to tell me what they'd done wrong, too. One little kid even offered to break another window for me.

I said, "No more broken windows, and listen closely. He got the twenty not because he broke the window, but because he had the guts to speak up, and he didn't know if he was going to get punished or what. This boy is going to go far! He made the decision to come forward no matter what. And that takes guts."

You see, it's like my Dad always told me. Our decisions are who we are. Decisions and having the guts to stick to our decisions against all odds. And in this story, my Dad, who was younger and weaker becomes the hero, and his older, stronger brother becomes the nobody. And that's how it works in real life, too. Bullies eventually become nobodies, and the persons who were tormented become "somebodies," if—and this is a big if—they only have the guts to endure and not get bitter.

So, in my opinion, this is, indeed, the greatest gift we can give to ourselves and God: to keep the faith and stretch ourselves to the stars as we reach inside ourselves with all our God-given power and magic.

Death of an Assassin

"The colonel is coming! The colonel is coming!" shouted a young, barefooted boy, running up the cobblestone street of the little settlement.

It was almost dark, and quickly Juan ran into his home, yelling, "Hurry, Mamá! Here comes *el coronel!*"

Emilia started screaming with terror. The last time the colonel and his men had caught them, they'd raped and beaten Emilia in front of Doña Margarita's very own eyes so that they, the Villaseñors, could see what became of anyone who refused to bow down to authority. But the great woman, Doña Margarita, had not shied away from her responsibilities. No, she'd knelt down and began to pray, refusing to close her eyes to the horrors that these abusive, federal troops put her daughter through. And she had watched them with her eyes wide open and prayed with her rosary in hand, asking God to forgive them and to not blame their mothers whose loins they came from.

Hearing Doña Margarita's words, one soldier had lost

his ability to rape Emilia, and he'd become so enraged with the old woman's praying that he'd pulled up his pants and rushed across the room to beat Doña Margarita. But another soldier had knocked him down. Then, in a fit of rage, the federal troops had begun to fight amongst themselves until the colonel had come in and separated them, calling them a bunch of weak fools because they didn't know how to properly treat a woman. The colonel had then yanked Doña Margarita's rosary from her hand and slapped her, calling her "a stupid Indian." And then he tore the rosary to pieces, scattering the well-worn beads to the wind.

Now Luisa and Doña Margarita quickly tried to get Emilia to stop screaming and ushered her out the back door of their home so they could hide in the bushes underneath the wall of the *ramada*. It was almost dark; there was just a little pink and pale yellow in the western sky painted across the heavens in soft, long horizontal brush strokes. The colonel and his men could be heard entering the village, their horses' hooves echoing on the rock-smooth cobblestones. Emilia began to cry again, whimpering like a lost little child. She wanted her doll. Ever since her last beating, nothing could pacify her except her dirty, little, ragged doll. It was a doll that she'd gotten as a child, ordered all the way from Spain, and at one time had been a wondrous Flamenco dancing woman with fine clothes and real blond hair.

"I'll run back inside and get it for her," said Salvador, his heart pounding in deadly fear.

"Oh, no, you don't!" said his mother. "They so much as see one little movement and they'll start shooting! You know how much they still fear us and hate us! No, you stay put!"

"But, Mamá," said Luisa, who was big with child, "if he

doesn't go and get her dirty little doll, they'll find us all and maybe even kill us this time. Please, let him go quickly before they get any closer and hear her."

Emilia was crying and whimpering, and the colonel and his troops were halfway up the street now. They were walking slowly, confidently, each horse stepping deliberately—well-shod horses and well-armed men coming down the cobblestones, watching every house, every shadow, as they came. They'd killed almost every male human down to the age of twelve in all the area, and so they figured that they had no one left to fear, fully realizing that the old men and little boys who were left had seen so much bloodshed in the last few years that their hearts were gone out of them.

"Mamá, Luisa is right," said Juan. He was ten years old and he'd been running and hiding and dodging bullets for the last three years of his life. "I've got to do it, and now!"

Quickly, he jumped up and sped out of the bushes, up over the wall, and across the *ramada*. The colonel and his men were only three houses up the street. He had to find his sister's doll and get back into hiding instantly or all would be lost. My God, he was so scared that his little heart was pounding a million miles an hour.

Going inside the house, he glanced all around the kitchen, but didn't see the doll. He rushed to the back, looking through the bed where Emilia and Luisa slept together. Ever since José-Luis' death, Luisa slept with Emilia. That way they could give each other comfort in the quiet of the night.

He found nothing. He rushed into the room where he and his mother slept on another straw mat on the floor. The last time the soldiers had come, they'd taken all their bedding and furniture and set it on fire in the street in front of their home. Oh, these soldiers were determined to show them what became of people who raised sons who dared feast their eyes on the Heavens and think of themselves as having value.

Searching desperately, Juan didn't find the doll there, either. Then he heard his sister's cries and the horses dancing, echoing, their well-shod hooves getting closer and closer. He just knew that they were going to be found. He rushed into the kitchen to get a pan or a knife to throw at the horseman, so that they'd give him chase and not find his mother and sisters. That's when he saw Emilia's doll. Why, it was sitting there on the ledge of the broken kitchen window with the last of the going sunlight reflecting off the doll's fine, smooth face.

Juan snatched up the doll and dashed out to the *ramada*, coming within a few feet of the well-shod horses' hooves. He dropped, crawling alongside the twisted vines of the *ramada*, his chest pounding against the good Earth. And he was just going to drop the doll over the rock wall to his mother and sisters when a soldier heard him and reined in his mount.

"What's that?" shouted the soldier, drawing his pistol and shooting once, twice, three times into the vines of the dark twisting *ramada*.

Hearing the shots, Doña Margarita and her daughters glanced up and saw Juan's hand hanging over the top of the wall above them. His hand opened, letting go of the doll, and then went limp. The old ragged dancing Flamenco woman came tumbling down through the leaves and branches of the bushes into Emilia's starving hands. Immediately, Emilia calmed down as if she'd been given a gift from Heaven. It took every ounce of power for Doña Margarita to not scream out in HORROR! Juan was dead. His hand had gone limp. They could now hear the colonel's huge, bellowing voice.

"Stop wasting your bullets, you fool!" snapped *el coronel*. "This village has nothing worth shooting anymore with our guns!"

The colonel's men laughed and continued down the cobblestone street, shooting now and then and laughing as they went. They'd won; the colonel figured that they'd killed each and every man, woman and child who'd seen him run down the road that night with his fat ass wiggling in awful fear. And anyone who might still be living, the colonel was sure that they wished that they were dead.

*   *   *

Late that night, little Pelón, Mateo's youngest brother, who'd given Juan his smooth, good-luck rock on the night of the witch, came to see Juan. The word was out that the federal troops had put three good bullet holes through Juan's body but that his mother, Doña Margarita, the great *curandera*, healer, had slipped the bullet holes from his body to his loose clothing and saved his life. Little Pelón found Juan and his family in the thick trees just down the hill from the town. They were going to sleep outside for a few nights in case the soldiers returned.

After inspecting the three bullet holes in Juan's clothing, just inches away from his neck and left side, Pelón informed

Juan that the last of his brothers had been assassinated two days before. "They came late in the day as we were eating, but we didn't run," said Pelón, tears coming to his eyes, "because I'm ten and Alfonso was only twelve, and they'd already killed Mateo and all my older brothers. So, well, my mother said, 'Don't run! Just keep eating and they'll leave us alone.' But they didn't. They shot Alfonso as he sat there eating his *taco de frijoles.*"

No one knew what to say. There'd been so much killing in the last couple of years that, my God, there seemed to be no end to it. As soon as a boy began to just show any little sign of manhood, he was executed on the spot. And the word was out that these killings would continue until every man, woman or child with any bad Indian blood was eradicated so that Mexico could then take its proper place among the modern nations of the world.

"Look," Pelón whispered to Juan once the women were asleep, "I've figured out a way to kill the colonel, but I need your help."

Juan glanced around, not wanting his mother and sisters to hear. He got up, and he and Pelón went out to the meadows beyond the trees. The moon was out and the sky was filled with thousands and thousands of stars. Facing each other, they sat down like two little dark stones, and Pelón explained the whole thing to Juan.

"You see, Juan, this is our only chance to do it," said Pelón, "now that *el coronel* figures that he's killed all of us and he's starting to use the same trails each time to come up here."

Juan nodded. He could see that it was a good plan and

the right time to do it, now that the colonel was so confident that he was leisurely coming up each time on the easy main trails. But, still, there was the problem of a weapon. Every pistol and rifle had long ago been confiscated by the Federales. There wasn't a weapon to be had in all the mountains.

"No, that's not true," said Pelón. "I saw where my brothers buried a couple of good rifles before they were killed." He stood up. "Are you in?"

Juan sat there on the ground, looking up at his childhood friend whom he had known since they'd begun to walk. "Yes," said Juan, standing up and taking hold of his friend's hand. "I'm in *a lo macho!*"

"*A lo macho!*" repeated Pelón, and he took Juan into his arms, hugging him. Two little boys, each ten years old, and each so scared and torn and worn that they didn't know what else to do.

"Look," added Pelón, wiping his eyes, "with you at my side, Juan, what can possibly go wrong? You're the one who faced La Bruja single-handedly and took three of the colonel's best bullets and didn't even lose a drop of blood! Nothing can go wrong, I tell you. It's done! Day after tomorrow, before the sun is chest high, *el coronel* will be dead, and this land will be free once again!"

And they held each other in a long *abrazo*, both knowing fully well that they really had not one chance in hell of pulling this off. But there was nothing else that they could do, for tomorrow they'd get a little hair on their upper lip or just a little bit taller, and then it would be their turn to be executed. Now, only while they were still children, did they have any chance whatsoever of succeeding.

*   *   *

Two days later, Juan met Pelón down in the deep gulleys
north of town. It was late afternoon; they only had a couple
more hours of good daylight.

"Did you tell anyone?" asked Pelón. Pelón, meaning
"bald-headed," had such a big, thick mane of wild hair that
everyone had teased him about his hair ever since he could
remember, saying that all the forests of the world would be
gone before Pelón went bald.

"No," said Juan. "I told no one."

"Not even your mother?" asked Pelón.

Juan resented this question. "Especially not my
mother!" he snapped. "My God, she'd be out of her head
with worry if I'd told her what we were about!"

"All right, calm down," said Pelón. "Calm down. I was
just checking. We can't be too careful with what we're about
to do."

"Did you get the rifle?" asked Juan.

"Sure. I got it over there in those rocks, wrapped in a
serape and covered with leaves."

Juan glanced over to the pile of large boulders and
could see nothing. He was glad that Pelón had hidden the
weapon well. After all, they didn't want to be seen lugging a
rifle around the countryside. He glanced back at Pelón.
There was something different about this childhood friend
of his; his eyes were not the eyes of a young boy anymore.

"Come," said Pelón, "we'll go over my plan once more.
You have Don Pío's blood in your veins, just like your
brother José, so you should have a head for strategy. Oh, my

brothers would marvel at José's strategy of battle. Our brothers, they were great, weren't they?" he added.

"Yes," said Juan. And he almost added, "If only they had lived." But he didn't say this. He held.

They went over to the boulders and hunched down out of sight, warmed a couple of *taquitos*, and ate as they spoke. The sun was finally going down, and they could soon travel without being seen.

Pelón's plan was simple. He'd been watching the federal troops for days now, and he'd come to realize that the colonel and his men were coming up from the lowlands on the same trail. And, every time, they'd rest their horses three-fourths of the way up the mountain in a little basin where there was water and grass. The colonel had also gotten in the habit of walking a little way away from his men to take a crap over a large, fallen log, from where he could keep watch on the trail above and below him.

"So, you see," Pelón had explained to Juan, "all we got to do is get there the night before and bury me in the dirt and cover me with leaves and broken branches. Then, in the morning, when he has his pants down and he's shitting, I'll just rise up and shoot him dead from a distance of about ten feet, so I'll be sure not to miss."

The plan could work, Juan was sure of it, if only he covered Pelón up correctly with the leaves and branches and the colonel came the same way and took his same crap and Pelón didn't lose his nerve.

"Look," said Juan, "I've been thinking your plan over very carefully, and I really do think that it can work. But, well, it's going to take a lot of nerve for you to stay there quietly all night and then to not panic or make a single move when the colonel and his men ride up, making so much noise and trampling all around you with their horses."

"I got the nerve," said Pelón. "Believe me, I got the nerve. After they killed Mateo and all my brothers, I've been thinking of nothing else but this!

"You know," he said, a strange calmness coming to his eyes, "*el coronel* is right. There isn't ever going to be peace in Mexico until they kill every one of us, damn their wretched souls!"

Juan was taken aback. He hadn't expected this hate, this power, this conviction, to come from one of his own playmates who was so young. But he could now see that he'd been kidding himself. For he, too, was raging mad inside, wanting to kill, to destroy this damned colonel and all his men. Oh, the abuses, the absolute horrors that these men had committed in the name of law and order were monstrous!

"All right," said Juan, "I agree with you that there isn't going to be peace in Mexico until somebody is killed, but it's not going to be us. It's them who must die. They don't work the fields, they don't protect their homes and families, so it's them who must go. We have to live as my brother José said. We, the meek, who give heart and soul and the sweat off our backs to our sacred piece of Earth."

"You're right," said Pelón. "And that's why we must do this. Let's go."

"Just wait," said Juan. "I want to see the rifle. Also, after I bury you, how will you know when to raise up and start shooting, especially if I bury you so well that you can't see and you can't be seen, either?"

Pelón was stumped. But not for long. "I guess I'll know to come up shooting when I hear his first shits and farts."

Both boys started laughing.

"Then, let's hope he eats well tonight and drinks a lot so he'll be shitting and farting big and loud tomorrow," added Juan, laughing all the more.

And so there they went, two little boys, lugging an old *retrocarga,* homemade shotgun, that hadn't been fired in years, to do in the most famous badmen of all the region. The sun was down now and the western sky was painted in long streaks of pink and rose and yellow and gold. The clouds were banked up against the distant mountain called El Serro Gordo, The Fat Mountain, and all the rolling little hills and valleys between that distant mountain and their own great mountain called El Serro Grande, The Big Mountain, were green and lush, looking so beautiful and peaceful.

The two little boys began to whistle as they went. They were absolutely stout-hearted in their belief that they would succeed, and so they were happy.

Overhead, the last of the great flocks of fork-tailed blackbirds came swooping by on their way to roost in the tall grasses by the shallow mountain lakes. It had been another good day on God's sacred Earth, and she, the Night, was now approaching in all her splendor and magic. The first few stars were beginning to make themselves known, shining brightly in the heavens. Oh, it was good to be alive, holding your head high and feasting your eyes upon the wondrous evening sky with your heart full of hope and glory.

*   *   *

No one knew where Juan was, and Doña Margarita was becoming very anxious. She wondered if her little son's disap-
pearance had anything to do with Pelón having come by the
night before. She decided to call Luisa back from looking for
Juan. She just had this little quiet feeling deep inside herself
that the two boys were up to something, and so maybe it
was best not to draw anymore attention to the fact that Juan
was missing.

Doña Margarita took in hand what was left of her father's once-fine handmade rosary and went outside to pray.
The sun was gone and the night was coming, and soon it
would be dark. Doña Margarita began to pray, releasing her
soul to God and knowing deep inside of herself that all
would turn out for the Sacred Good, if only she kept faith
and allowed God to do His work, and let herself bend with
the turns and twists of life, and not take too seriously those
fears that kept coming up inside her weak, human mind.
For she well knew that the turns and twists of life could
never be understood with the head, but had to be felt by the
heart and allowed to blossom with the wisdom of one's God-
given soul.

Oh, if it weren't for her complete faith in God, she was
sure that she never could've survived that terrible day that
the colonel and his men had abused Emilia. But, with her
feet well-planted in the rich soil of the Mother Earth, she
had endured and she'd been able to go on, just as she was
going to go on now. This was the power of living; this was
the power of bringing in God's light with every breath one
took. To fill one's being with so much light that no little,
dark, sneaky thought of fear or doubt could reside in one's
entire being.

Doña Margarita now continued praying, eyes focused on the Father Sky and feet planted in the Mother Earth, not really knowing where her little boy was, but fully realizing that her soul was gone from her body, having been released to God's infinite powers, and her soul would somehow find the means with which to help her son. She prayed and the Universe listened and the stars brightened.

*   *   *

Going down through the trees, the two boys dropped into the little basin. It was dark now, and they needed to move slowly, carefully, and not leave any signs of having passed through there. Grass was in the open places and leaves and broken branches were under the trees. Then, they heard a sound. They froze, not moving a muscle, and glanced around, but only with their eyes—barely moving their heads or bodies.

Two eyes were watching them from over there by two trees. They couldn't quite make out what the two eyes were until they saw the flicker of the ears. Then they knew that it was a deer. In fact, they could now make out that it was a doe and her fawn, which had stepped out from behind her.

"*Mira, mira,*" said Pelón, blowing out with relief. Both boys had been holding their breath in deadly fear. "I thought maybe it was a tiger, or maybe even a soldier. You know, if the colonel was smart," continued Pelón, "he would leave a group of soldiers behind to keep track of their trails. That's what I'll do when I join Villa," he added with *gusto*.

"You're going to join Pancho Villa?" asked Juan, also feeling relieved that it had turned out to be only a deer.

"Sure, of course. It's either join the rebels or continue to stay up here all alone in these God-forsaken mountains until they hunt us all down. It's not going to stop with us killing the colonel, you know. They'll be sending others."

"Well, then, why are we doing this?" asked Juan. He'd assumed that once they'd gotten rid of *el coronel* it would all be over.

"Because the BAS . . ." Pelón began shouting in anger.

Just then, the doe leaped, looking behind her, and was off in large, graceful bounds. Her fawn went right after her in small, tight prancing leaps. Both boys crouched down, holding deadly still. They couldn't see what had startled the doe, but they were terrified once again. Pelón signaled Juan to follow him, and they moved quietly along the ground, their little hearts beating wildly.

Crawling into the brush, they lay down, chests against the good Earth. Juan drew close to Pelón's right ear and whispered, "Look, maybe we shouldn't bury you right now. I think maybe we should wait until daybreak, when we can see better. That doe was really frightened."

"Maybe it was just because I raised my voice," said Pelón.

"Maybe," said Juan, "but maybe not. I think we should wait."

"I don't know," whispered Pelón. "They've been coming by here pretty early."

"Yes, but what if the situation doesn't look right in the morning? Once you're buried, Pelón, that's it. We can't just uncover you. I think we better wait until daylight so we can see. Then I can bury you carefully and fix up the area so it looks like nobody has been here."

Pelón glanced around, thinking over the situation, then

said, "Okay, I'll trust your judgment, Juan, but I just hope he doesn't come by too early and catch us sleeping."

"He won't," said Juan. "Remember, he's going to eat and drink a lot tonight, so he'll fart big and loud for us tomorrow!"

Both boys laughed quietly, trying hard to keep their voices down. They still didn't know what had startled the doe, and they wanted to be very careful.

"You know," said Juan, glancing up at the star-studded heavens, "I think we should maybe pray."

"You still pray," asked Pelón, "after all that's happened to our families?"

At first Juan was taken aback by Pelón's question, but then he recovered and said, "Yes, of course. In fact, at home we probably pray more now than ever before." And so Juan knelt there in the brush where they were hiding and began to pray, with Pelón only watching. Overhead the stars continued blinking, winking, giving wonderment and beauty.

"Come on," said Juan to Pelón, "join me. In the morning, we'll have plenty of time to do everything."

"All right," said Pelón. "I hope you're right."

And so now, both boys were praying together. The doe came back down into the grassy meadow and began to graze once again. Whatever had frightened her was gone now. Upon seeing the doe and her fawn return, the boys felt better and finished up their prayers, feeling good and confident once again.

"And so, *buenas noches,* dear God," said Juan, finishing his prayer, "and let us sleep in peace and keep us well throughout the night."

"And help us tomorrow," added Pelón, "that we not fail,

for we are pure of heart and only wish to protect our homes and families."

Making the sign of the cross over themselves, the two boys came out from the brush and stood up in the clearing by the doe and her little fawn. It was a magnificent night, filled with thousands of bright stars and not a single cloud. The doe and her fawn looked at the two small boys, but didn't bolt. The two animals seemed very much at peace once again.

"I wonder," said Juan, "if animals pray, too. Look how relaxed and happy they are now."

"Animals don't pray," said Pelón, laughing. "What are you, *loco*?"

"No," said Juan, "my mother has always told us that praying calms the heart, and look how peaceful those deer are now."

Pelón glanced at the deer and then back at Juan. "Did your mother really move those bullet holes from your body to your clothes? You know, everyone is starting to say that your mother is the real *bruja* of our region, but that she's a good witch because she goes to church every day."

"My mother is no *bruja*!" snapped Juan.

"Look, I didn't mean to offend you," said Pelón. "It's just that, well, did she move those bullets from your body to your clothes?"

Juan didn't want to answer. He'd been out cold when they'd taken him inside. "I don't know," he said. "I was told that the one bullet hit so close to my head that I was knocked out. But, yes, that's what they were saying when I came to. They said that they'd seen the other two bullets in my body, and I was dead until my mother lit the candles and put her hands on me and started praying."

"Then your mother really is a witch," said Pelón, making the sign of the cross over himself, eyes large with wonder.

"No, she isn't!" said Juan. "Women just come from the moon—you know that. And, well, when they show their power, and the men see that they can't move them, people start calling them witches. But they're not. They're just women, damn it! My mother is no witch! Not any more than yours!"

"Don't call my mother a witch!" yelled Pelón.

"Well, then, don't call mine one, either. Hell, your mother has done wonders, too. No one can figure out how she keeps your corn growing, even after the soldiers trample and burn it."

Pelón calmed down. "All right," he said, "you're right. My mother does wonders, too, so I won't call your mother, well, a *bruja* anymore. But tell me, Juan, how come you know so much about all this?" asked the boy, his eyes still huge with fear. "You aren't a brujo, are you?"

"Of course not," said Juan, getting really tired of the whole subject. "It's just that each night when my mother puts us to bed, she tells us stories."

"What kind of stories?"

"Well, stories about the magic of life. Stories that give us hope and strength, wings of understanding, so no matter how awful the world gets all around us, we'll always still feel the power of God's breath . . . giving us light, just like those stars and moon give light to the darkness."

"I see," said Pelón. "I see. Just like those stars and moon, eh?"

"Yes," said Juan. "Just like those stars and moon."

The fawn had come closer to the two boys. It was obvious that Pelón still wasn't too sure about Juan and had a thousand more questions, but Juan wanted no more of this. He was exhausted. Ever since that soldier had shot at him, everyone had been asking him what his mother had done to him and if it was true that she'd brought him back from the dead.

"I'm tired," said Juan. "I think we better find a place to bed down for the night so we can go to sleep.

"Look, the little fawn wants to smell us," added Juan, smiling and putting his hand out to the little deer. The fawn stretched out his neck, sniffing Juan's fingertips. "You know, I bet animals really do pray in their own way," said Juan. "That's how they're able to live surrounded by lions and all these other dangers but still live in such peace and happiness."

"Maybe you're right," said Pelón, feeling that no deer would come this close to a real witch because wild animals—it was well-known—could see what lurked inside a human's heart. "Come on, I'm tired, too. Let's go over to that huge tree by the fallen log where the colonel does his *caca* and find a place to sleep."

"Okay," said Juan, getting to his feet slowly. He didn't want to startle the little deer.

Both boys now went over to the huge tree by the fallen log where the colonel had been relieving himself each time he came up the mountain. They got down between the thick, bare roots of the tree that some pigs had uprooted, creating a little hollow. They wanted to get out of the wind and cold so that they could get a good night's rest.

The fawn, who'd been watching them, saw them disappear into the hollow and came over to see what had happened to them. The doe followed her fawn and saw the two boys going to sleep. She took up ground, standing over the boys and her fawn like a sentry.

Juan remembered opening his eyes once and seeing the mother deer standing over them, and he just knew that his mother had come to protect them in the form of a mother deer. But he didn't say anything about this to Pelón. He didn't want to confuse things any more than they already were. High overhead, the stars were blinking, winking by the thousands, and the moon gave her magic light, too. It had been another good day and now it was becoming a good night. There were no witches or other evils on the other side. No, there was just the fear and jealousy that people took with them in their souls.

"Buenas noches," said Juan to the miracle of the heavens. "And thank you, Mamá," he said to the mother deer. He breathed more easily and went back to sleep, feeling safe, and dreamed of green meadows and happy deer praying to the Almighty.

*　　*　　*

The two boys were fast asleep when they first heard the snorts of the colonel's horses coming up the steep grade. Quickly, they opened their eyes, not knowing what to do. Oh, my God, they'd been caught with their pants down. And now they couldn't just jump up and take off running or they'd be spotted and shot down for sure. They glanced at each other, then raised up their heads as much as they dared and looked between the displaced tree roots. They saw that the soldiers were already in the basin. Some were already off their horses and putting them to graze. Others were taking their mounts down to the water to drink. Then, they heard the colonel's big, powerful voice and realized that he was directly behind them. But they didn't dare turn around to look.

"Take my horse!" shouted *el coronel*, belching loudly. He sounded like a man with a bad stomach. "Over there, over there. Get the hell away from me!"

They could hear the soldier doing as he was told, grabbing the reins of the colonel's horse and quickly leading him off, coming so close to them that they could see the horse's hooves passing by as they looked from under the big roots of the huge tree. Then, here came the colonel himself, passing by them even closer, his tall, leather boots glistening in the early morning light. He was grabbing tree branches as he passed, causing leaves to fall, and belching with every step. Oh, he was in terrible shape. They could smell the sour odor coming off of him.

Juan and Pelón glanced at each other and, if they hadn't been so terrified, they would've burst out laughing. This was exactly what they'd wanted. They couldn't have asked for it any better. Then, there was the colonel, only fifteen feet away from them, unbuckling his gun belt and dropping his pants. He turned away from them and barely got his big white ass over the fallen log before he began to shit with enormous-sounding explosions.

Quickly, Pelón reached under himself, bringing up the rifle, which was still wrapped in the serape. He tried to unwrap the weapon as quickly and quietly as he could, but he was having trouble working within the small confines of the little hollow.

Juan kept glancing at the colonel, praying to God, "Oh, please, dear God," he said to himself, "let him be so full of farts and caca that he doesn't stop shitting and can't hear us!"

Finally, Pelón had the weapon uncovered, but it was pointing in the wrong direction. Quickly, he tried turning it around, hitting Juan in the face with the barrel.

Seeing the huge barrel of the homemade retrocarga, Juan blurted out, "That's it? That's our weapon?"

"Quiet!" whispered Pelón under his breath as he shoved the huge weapon between the roots, pointing it at the colonel's back side.

"But it won't shoot!" said Juan. "I thought we had a real rifle!"

But Pelón wasn't paying attention to Juan anymore, and he now cocked back the two big hammers and spoke out loud. *"Coronel,"* he said in a clear, good voice, "I'm Mateo's little brother!"

And, as the colonel turned to see who had the audacity to come up behind him and bother him while he relieved himself, Pelón pulled both triggers. But nothing happened; the hammers just didn't move.

Instantly, the colonel saw the situation: two little boys with an old retrocarga from the days of Benito Juárez, hunched down under a bunch of big tree roots, trying to kill him. Quick as a cat, he pulled up his pants and reached for his gun belt. But, at that very instant, Juan hit the two hammers with a stone, and the old weapon EXPLODED, pipe-barrel splitting in two and a fountain of rock and used little pieces of iron shooting toward the colonel. The two boys were thrown back with the explosion of the weapon, smashing Pelón against the dirt across the hollow. The colonel was thrown over backwards across the log. Instantly, his men were shouting and taking cover, returning fire.

Crawling out of the hollow, Juan was up and trying to clear his head so they could take off running. But what he saw Pelón do next was something he'd never forget. Pelón didn't run. No, he cleared his head and ran over to the colonel, who was squirming about in terrible pain, took the colonel's gun from his gun belt and emptied the pistol into his naked, bloated belly. The soldiers' bullets sang all around Pelón's head, but he never gave them any importance. Only when he saw that the great bad man was dead did Pelón throw down the gun and come running toward Juan. Then they were off like deer, running down through the brush and trees as the soldiers continued shooting at them.

"I killed him!" yelled Pelón, as they ran. "I killed him and he looked me in the eyes and knew who I was before he died! Oh, it was wonderful!"

Some of the soldiers got on their horses and tried to give chase, but the two boys knew these mountains like the back of their hands and cut through the breaks, leaping from boulder to boulder, leaving the armed men far behind. Finally, they were down in the deep canyons where the wild orchids grew, and they were going to start back up the mountainside when they came upon the doe and her little fawn once again. The deer had been bedded down.

"Wait," said Juan. "Maybe this is a good place for us to

hole up for the day. We don't want to get up on top and run into the soldiers or someone who might turn us in to them."

"Who'd turn us in?" asked Pelón. He was so excited that he was ready to pop. "I killed him! I killed him! Oh, my God, it was wonderful! Seeing him squirm around, I put a bullet into his fat belly for every one of my brothers! We did it, Juan! We really did it!"

"Yes, we did. But now we got to keep calm so we don't get killed, too. Come, let's get up on that ridge and bed down like the deer do and keep very quiet 'til nighttime."

And they'd no more than hidden themselves when here came five mounted soldiers down into the bottom of the canyon with an old Indian leading them on foot. The two boys held their breath, watching them pass by down below in the trees. Once, the Indian stopped and glanced up in their direction, but then he just went on down the canyon bottom, leading the soldiers away.

"Did you see how *el indio* looked up toward us?" asked Pelón.

"Yes," said Juan. "He knows we're up here. We better go before they circle above us and come in from behind."

The two boys took off up the ridge as fast as they could go, startling the doe and her fawn, who'd bedded down above them.

"You better run, too!" said Juan to the deer as they went racing by them.

But the deer didn't run with them. Instead, they ran downhill. Juan and Pelón were coming off the top of the ridge when they heard the shooting down below.

Juan stopped. "They shot the deer," he said.

"How do you know?" asked Pelón.

"I just know," said Juan, tears coming to his eyes.

And he took off racing for home as fast as he could go. He had to see if his beloved dear old mother was all right.

Two days later, Pelón disappeared. It was rumored that he'd joined Francisco Villa's army and had been given the rank of Captain, making him the youngest officer Villa had ever welcomed into his armed forces.

*   *   *

Author's Note

In real life, Rambo and John Wayne and Schwarzenegger and all these other big fake movie heroes have it all backwards. It doesn't take big muscles and all these modern guns to be a Superman or Superwoman. That's all superficial bull! It's not how big the dog is, but how big the fight in the dog is.

And each one of us, no matter how small or young, can defend ourselves once we set our mind to it. Conviction of heart is our power. Truly, conviction of heart, making that "decision" that this is it and we are going to do it, no matter what. Why, this colonel had killed well over five hundred people, and he'd bullied thousands of others, entire communities, and yet these two little boys did him in. No one, but no one, can push people too far. Even the most meek and good-of-heart will finally stand up and be accounted for.

Also, my father and his friend didn't do this for glory or medals or to prove anything to anyone. No, they did it for the love of their families, the love that they had for their mothers and sisters and little brothers and their sacred piece of Mother Earth.

Thank you. *Gracias*. We're all somebody, people of value. All we have to do is make that "decision" to stand up and do it!

Toreando el tren
or
Bullfighting the Train

In the next few days, Juan met many boys his own age as they waited alongside the railroad tracks. There were boys from all over the Republic of Mexico, and they were on their way north to the United States with their families, escaping the Mexican Revolution.

A few of the boys liked to gamble, so Juan set up foot races with them to see who was the fastest, and they threw rocks to see who was the strongest. And Juan, who was eleven and had always thought he was pretty strong and fast, lost most of the contests.

Many of these boys were really powerful, especially the full-blooded Tarascan Indians from the State of Michoacán. In fact, Juan figured that some of them were probably as good as his long-legged brother, Domingo, who'd been five years older than him and one of the fastest and strongest boys in all their region of Los Altos de Jalisco.

Domingo and Juan had been closest in age and they'd been raised together. Juan missed Domingo dearly. He'd disappeared just two months before they'd left their beloved mountains. But their mother still thought that there was a good chance that maybe Domingo was alive and hadn't been killed, like all his other older brothers.

Juan and his newly-found friends played up and down the tracks and through the burned-out buildings, pretending to be Pancho Villa and Emiliano Zapata and other heroes of the Revolution. They were mostly nine, ten and eleven years old, and they just couldn't wait for the day when they'd be big enough so they, too, could take up arms.

Juan told the boys of the different incidents of war that he'd seen up in his mountainous region of Los Altos, and how brave and courageous his brothers and uncles had been.

Hearing Juan's stories, the other boys told their stories, too, and little by little Juan grew to understand that either these boys were huge liars or in other parts of Mexico they'd truly had it much worse than his family had it up in their isolated mountains.

For not until the last year had the war really hit them up in Los Altos de Jalisco. Before that, José, Juan's greatest brother, and a handful of local boys had managed to keep their mountains free of war, just as Don Pío and his Rural Police had managed to keep them free of bandit gangs years before.

"*Mira!*" yelled Juan, hitting his legs with a stick. "I'm the famous Four-White-Stockings stallion of my brother's! And here come five hundred horsemen after me, but I jump across the *barranca,* and they all fall to their death!"

"Me, too!" said another boy, named Eduardo. "I'm the

great Villa! And here I come to help you, Juan, with my Dorados del Norte—the finest horsemen of the earth!"

"Oh, no, they're not!" said a third boy, named Cucho. "General Obregón's cavalry led by Colonel Castro are the finest!"

"Hey, that's my cousin!" said Juan excitedly. "On my mother's side! My Great Uncle Agustín's fifth son!"

"But I thought you were for Villa!" said Eduardo. He was almost twelve and the strongest of them all.

"I am!" said Juan. "But I'm also for my cousin! How can I not be, eh?"

The boys played and challenged each other, throwing stones and racing. Then it was the day for Juan and his family to go north. They got on the train along with the thousands of other people, getting in one of the tall empty cattle cars. But the floor of the car was so full of cow manure that they had to get back out and shovel all the *caca* out by hand before they could find a place to sit down for the long ride north.

But, they'd no more settled in and the train started moving, when Juan got up and sneaked out of the boxcar along with five of his new friends.

The day before, Juan and Eduardo and Cucho and three other boys had made a bet among themselves to see who was the bravest of them all. The bet was to see who would stay alongside the tracks as the train took off and be the last one to run and jump on the train.

They called this *toreando* the train, or bullfighting the train, and all six boys realized that this was a very risky game because, if they didn't catch the train and they got separated from their families, it could be for life.

Juan's heart was pounding with fear as he now stood alongside the tracks and watched the huge iron-wheels of the train turning slowly in front of him, carrying the long row of cars down the tracks. He watched the train weighted down with people, stuffed full in the boxcars, piled high with their bags and boxes on the flatbeds. His heart went wild, but still he held and he watched people holding on every which way they could so they could get to the safety of the north. Juan was full of the devil; he just knew this was one event.

After all, he was a Villaseñor with Castro blood, and all week long these boys had been outdoing him in throwing rocks and running foot races. But now he'd show them in one great, swift challenge what he was truly made of. For he, Juan, was the boy who'd gotten a man's reputation up in his mountainous region at the age of six years old when he'd proved himself to be so brave that it was said that his blood ran backwards from his heart.

Oh, he'd never forget that night. It had been a full moon and the local witch had put a curse on his family. So it was up to the youngest, who was purest of heart, to redeem *la familia.* And he'd done it.

Licking his lips, Juan glanced at his friends as the train started moving a little faster. He felt like a bantam rooster. After all, he had the blood of his grandfather, Don Pío, running through his veins.

"Getting scared, eh?" said Eduardo to Juan as the train slipped past them. He was the oldest and strongest of them all and the second-fastest runner.

"Not me," said Juan.

"Nor I," said Cucho.

The big iron wheels were turning faster, crying metal to metal as the long line of boxcars and flatbeds went by. Five thousand people were going out that day, and there wouldn't be another empty train going north for weeks.

Juan's heart began to pound. Oh, how he wished these boys would just get scared and run for the train so he, too, could run after his family.

The huge iron wheels turned faster and faster. A part of Juan's mind started telling him to stop this ridiculous game and jump forward and get on the train to join his mother while he still had the chance. But he wouldn't move. No, he just held there alongside the other boys, refusing to be the first one to give in.

The sounds of the big turning, sliding, moving iron wheels on the shiny-smooth steel rails were getting louder and louder. The huge long train—well over fifty units and two locomotives—was picking up speed. Finally, one of the younger boys couldn't stand it anymore and he screamed out.

"I'm going!" He leaped forward, catching one of the passing boxcars and swung on.

"He wants his *mamá*!" laughed the boys.

Juan and the other boys laughed at him, saying that he was a cowardly little baby.

Why, the end of the train hadn't even slid by them yet, so they ridiculed this boy. But still, down deep inside their souls they all knew that he'd done the right thing and they all wanted to be with their *mamás*, too.

Then here came the end of the train, coming by them at a good pace, but still not going so fast that a good runner couldn't catch it. Juan grinned, feeling good. Now it truly took guts not to cry out and run. So there went the end of the train, cranking iron to iron past Juan's face. It left him and all the other boys behind, going up the long, desolate valley. A second boy now cried out in fear.

"This is stupid!" he screamed. "We could lose our families forever!"

He took off running after the end of the train and swung on. Once more Juan and the boys who'd remained behind laughed, calling this other boy a coward, too.

"Well, I guess this only leaves us, the real *hombres*!" said Juan, watching the train beginning to pick up speed as it went up the long, flat valley.

"Yeah, I guess so," said Cucho, "but at least I'm the fastest runner, so I can afford to wait. I don't know what you other slowpokes are doing here. It's four days by horseback to the next town."

And saying this, he suddenly took off running up the track. He, Cucho, the fastest boy among them. Juan wanted to scream out in fear, but he didn't. He held strong. He had to. He was from Los Altos de Jalisco, after all.

"Darn Cucho," said Eduardo, who'd been left behind with Juan and another boy, "trying to scare us. Heck, a good man can always outwalk any train. All you need is water."

"Right," said Juan, trying to act like he, too, wasn't scared. But inside he was ready to pee in his pants, he was so terrified. "With water, a good man can always survive," he added.

Juan held there alongside the two tall, lanky Indian boys, but it was hard. Juan was beginning to lose the power inside himself. He wasn't one of the fastest runners, after all. And the train was getting farther down the tracks.

Then another boy took off. He was tall and fast, but, still, he was having an awful time catching the train. He held on to his hat, running as fast as he could, arms swinging, bare feet lifting, and got up close to the end of the going train. But he just couldn't get a hold.

Juan glanced at Eduardo next to him.

"Hey," he said, "we even outwaited Cucho, the fastest of all, so I think we've shown our worth!"

"Yeah, let's go!"

"Yeah!" said Juan. "We've both won!"

So they both took off down the tracks and, in the distance, the last boy finally got hold of the train. He tried to swing up, but he lost his footing and his legs almost went under the steel wheels.

Seeing this, Juan screamed out in terror and ran with all his might, arms pumping, feet climbing, having run up and down mountains all his life. He ran and ran, gaining on the train, but the pace was killing him.

But then the front end of the long train hit a small downward grade. Suddenly, the whole train jerked forward, picking up speed. Eduardo gave it all he had, pulling ahead of Juan.

Juan saw the train going and he thought of his mother and his sister. He could imagine the grief and terror in his mother's old face when she discovered that he wasn't on the train and she'd lost yet another child. Tears came to his eyes and he got more scared than he'd ever been in all his life.

"*Mamá! Mamá!*" he cried out in anguish.

He raced on with all his heart and soul. The people on top of the boxcars looked back and saw the two boys running after them. But they thought they were only local boys playing, so they just waved.

Gripped with the sudden understanding that he'd lost his mother forever, Juan lost all hope, and he tripped, falling face-first into the sharp rocks between railroad ties and ripped open his mouth.

He lay there spitting blood and choking, and his eyes flowed with tears. The tall, lanky Indian, who'd gotten a good fifteen yards ahead of him, came walking back slowly.

The long train was gone now. It was a good quarter of a mile down the tracks, whistling and picking up more and more speed as it went north from the city of León toward Aguascalientes, Zacatecas, and Gómez Palacio, where it was supposed to stop over for the night and refuel before going on to Chihuahua and then Ciudad Juárez across the Rio Grande from El Paso, Texas, in the United States.

Coming back, Eduardo saw that Juan was all bloody and he offered him his hand.

"Well," said Juan, getting to his feet and wiping the blood from his face, "let's go! We got to catch that train!"

"Don't be crazy, *mano*," said the tall, lanky boy in a relaxed manner. "Not even a horse could catch it now."

"But we got to," said Juan desperately. "Our families are on that train!"

"Yes," said the tall boy casually, "that's true. But I also have an uncle and aunt back here in León, so I can always catch the next train."

"You mean you still have family back here?" screamed Juan, suddenly getting so raging mad that all fear was gone.

"Well, yes," said the boy, not knowing why Juan was getting so upset.

"Well, then you lied!" screamed Juan. "You tricked me! You didn't make your bet with your whole family on the train!"

The boy only laughed. "Well, no, of course not, *mano*," he said. "Only a fool would bet everything."

"You . . . you . . . !" said Juan.

"Eh, don't swear at me or I'll beat you, Juan. I'm the strongest boy among us, remember? You wouldn't have a chance."

"I spit on your strength!" said Juan to the bigger, older boy. "I'll fight you to the death right now! Come on, let's do it like the devil painted it!"

Seeing Juan's insane rage, the larger boy backed off. "Eh, *mano*, I'm sorry," he said. "Look, you can come and stay with me and my family until we go."

"Stick your family in your pocket!" said Juan. "I'm catching that train!" He picked up his hat and turned, taking off down the tracks.

The train was so far away now that it looked like nothing more than a small dark line, smoking in the distance as it headed for the far end of the long flat valley. Way ahead of the train, Juan could see a bunch of little red-rock hills no bigger than fresh cow-pies, but he didn't lessen his pace. His mother, his most perfect love in all the world, was on that train. So he'd run to the end of the earth if he had to.

*   *   *

The sun was high and Juan talked to God as he went, stepping quickly from tie to tie. He didn't want to wear out the bottoms of his worn-out *huaraches* on the crushed sharp rocks between the wooden ties.

"Oh, dear God," said Juan, watching the tar-painted ties slide under his feet as he went, "I know I've sinned many times in the past, but I swear to You that I'll never sin again if You help me this time. Give me the wings of an angel so I can fly across this land and catch the train. For remember, You're all-powerful and can do whatever You please and, besides, it's not just me who'll suffer if I die, dear God. It will be my beloved mother who loves You more than life itself!"

And saying this, Juan smiled as he ran on. He liked how he'd added his mother there at the end, and he hoped it would make God feel guilty and force Him to come through and give him the wings of an angel.

But the wings didn't come, so he kept running, eating up the miles. And to his surprise, instead of getting weaker and weaker, he got stronger.

The morning passed by and Juan noticed that the railroad men had cheated and started putting the ties farther apart. He began to miss the wooden ties as he ran, hitting the sharp rocks instead. Juan's *huaraches* came apart and twice he had to stop to fix them with a piece of his shirt. He began to get thirsty and thick-tongued, but there were no signs of water anywhere.

"Oh, Mamá," he said, glancing up at the great white sun, "what have I done to us? Without water, even a good man from Los Altos can't survive.

"Oh, dear God," he said, "Lord and Master of all the Heavens, forgive me, for I'm a fool. And I know that I played around and gambled when I should have been serious. But . . . well, if You help me this time, dear God, and give me the wings of—look, if it's bothering You to make me an angel because I've never been that good—then how about the wings of an eagle, and I swear to You that I will never gamble or play around again when I should be serious."

So Juan talked to God, his Old Companion, who'd helped him all his life. The miles went by and the sun grew hotter and hotter. But not once did he slow down.

He was strong; he'd been raised in the mountains at nearly six thousand feet, and ever since he could remember, he'd been running from sun-to-sun with his brother Domingo and their giant cousins, Basilio and Mateo, chasing the wolves and coyotes away from their herds of goats.

But it was hotter down here in the valley. Juan was sweating more than he was used to. The powerful sun grew larger and larger and the high desert insects began to screech. Once, way ahead in the distance, Juan thought he saw a group of green trees. He figured it had been a water hole.

"Oh, thank You, God," he said, and his mouth began to water, feeling better as he approached the trees.

But then, getting there, he saw that the water hole had long ago dried up. Why, even in the shade of the trees, the earth was nothing but dead-cracked skin.

"Oh, God!" he screamed. "Why do You tease me?"

And he thought he'd die, he was so thirsty. But then he remembered his mother and how she'd lost child after child in the Revolution and he stopped his rage. He had to be strong for her. He glanced around. He saw the little red hills. They were much bigger now. He looked back. The city of León was nothing but a wrinkle in the distance.

"I can make it," he said, taking courage. "I know I can."

He rested a few moments in the shade of the trees along

with a few lizards and a fat reddish rattlesnake. Then he took off once again, but this time at an easy-going dog-trot.

The sun, the blanket of the poor, continued its journey across the tall, flat sky, and the day grew so hot that the black tar on the railroad ties melted and came off on his huaraches. Heat waves danced in the distance and mirages of huge blue lakes glistened all around.

Juan became so thirsty that his mouth turned to cotton and his vision blurred. Finally, he began to walk. He started talking to himself so he wouldn't go crazy. He remembered the stories that his mother had told him of his grandfather, the great Don Pío, and of his two brothers, Cristóbal and Agustín.

Time passed and the insects grew louder and the sun grew hotter, and Juan concentrated way back to those wonderful days up in Los Altos de Jalisco before the Revolution had come to them. He smiled, feeling good, remembering how cool and green the meadows of his youth had been. He smiled and began to trot and thought back to those days of his youth when he and his brother had played with Basilio and Mateo, the two sons of their Great Uncle Cristóbal.

Oh, those were the days! Playing with those huge, dark Indian-looking men who'd even towered over their father, who was a very big man. Juan ran on. Why, they'd had heavy-boned Indian faces and small yellowish teeth, and they'd been well into the age of wisdom when Juan had first started playing with them. But still, they'd been as simple as children, refusing to live indoors and, instead, had slept under the oak leaves when the weather got cold.

They wouldn't come inside when it rained, but, instead, they loved to race and dance and shout to the Heavens every time it stormed. They had no sense of money or personal property and would give away anything that anyone asked them for. They never rode a horse or a burro, but, instead, would challenge any horseman to a race across that meadow, over that ridge, and to that distant *barranca*. And they almost always won, even against the fastest horses, because they knew the mountains like the fingers of their hands. And even though many people called them simple, everyone knew that they were not fools.

Oh, he was feeling good now, running up the tracks at a good dog-trot, thinking of his two giant cousins. And no, he would never forget the day that he'd seen his two great cousins follow an armadillo into a cave where they'd found a chest of gold so big that a burro couldn't carry it. Oh, that had been such a wonderful day, taking the mountain of gold home to Don Pío and his Uncle Cristóbal.

*   *   *

The bottoms of Juan's *huaraches* were gone. The rocks were poking up between them and getting caught in the leather straps. Sitting down on the iron rail, Juan took off his *huaraches* and decided he'd probably be better off barefoot. But walking on the ties, his feet got stuck to the boiling-hot, half-melted tar. He found he was better off going on the sharp stones between the ties.

"Oh, Basilio," he said aloud as he limped along, "if only you and Mateo were here right now to put me on your shoulders and run with me like you used to do when I was a boy." His eyes filled with tears. "But don't worry," he said. "I'm not giving up. Your blood is my blood!"

And saying this, he started loping once again, flying over

the stones with his bare feet. He could almost feel his giant cousins here beside him. He'd loved them and they'd loved him and so they'd always be here inside him, giving him strength, giving wings to his feet. He raced on.

The sun inched its way across the towering flat, blue sky and the little red-rock hills continued dancing between the heat waves in the distance. Juan remembered the day that his brother, Domingo, had finally become so big that he thought he could beat Basilio and Mateo in a foot race.

Boys from all over the mountains came to see. The race was set up in the green meadow by the three lakes.

"But wait," said Basilio. "I don't race for free no more. Every month some new boys want to challenge me and my brother. We got to get paid."

"How much?" said Domingo. He was hot. He really wanted to beat them.

"Well, I don't know," said Basilio, his eyes dancing with merriment. "But my brother and I were talking and, well, we figure that we never had enough peanuts to fill our bellies, so we'd like a sack of peanuts."

"Jesus Christ!" screamed Domingo. "That would cost a fortune!"

Basilio and Mateo roared. But Domingo wanted to race, and so he stole one of their father's goats and traded it for a twenty-kilo sack of peanuts.

The marks were set, Domingo and the two giants got in place, and then the call was made and they were off. And Domingo, blue-eyed and red-headed like his father, took off like lightning, barefoot and stripped to the waist. The muscles on his back rippled as his legs and arms worked so fast they became a blur of motion. He was flying, sailing over the short green meadow grass. But he never had a chance. For he'd gone no more than ten yards when the two giants went racing past him, each carrying a young calf on their backs like they always did when they raced against human beings and not against horses. They leaped over the short rock fence at the end of the meadow and began to dance with the *gusto* of children.

Oh, those were the days! Domingo had gotten so mad that his face had become as red as the setting sun. Everyone laughed at him, but he had to admit that he was still a long way from ever beating the giants in a race.

Basilio and Mateo had shared their twenty-kilo sack of peanuts with all of them. They'd had other races between the younger boys and then they'd eat the peanuts—shells and all—so they could fill their starving furnaces of youth.

Juan ran on, feeling tired, drained, exhausted. But he never once lessened his pace. He had his grandfather, Don Pío, in his soul. He had his cousins, Basilio and Mateo, in his legs. And his brothers, Domingo and José, were in his heart. And his mother—the greatest woman in all the world—was waiting for him up ahead. He ran on.

*   *   *

The sun was blasting hot and the valley was flat and wide and filled with nothing but dead, dry brush. He licked his lips, but found that he had no saliva. So he stopped, picked up a small stone, and wiped it off. He put it in his mouth to suck on. Oh, he'd never forget the day of the race that they'd also bought a basket of oranges and he'd tasted his first orange. They'd cut one into quarters and he'd seen the luscious slices, juice dripping down, golden and wet and as sweet as honey. He'd eaten three big oranges that day and he'd felt strong.

Running up the valley, still tasting the sweet-wetness of that golden orange, he now saw that the sun was beginning to slide down the tall, flat sky. Why, he'd run all day without really realizing it. *El ojo de Dios,* the eye of God, was going down and the long, dark shadows of the coming night engulfed him as he came up to the first little hills. He'd made it across the valley with the help of his family: powerful men and women whose belief in God was so strong that life was indestructible.

He stopped. His feet were swollen and bloody. He wondered if he couldn't find some water here in these little hills and stay for the night before going on.

Looking back, he saw that he must have been climbing for the last hour. The long, flat valley now lay way down below him. There were no traces of León, not even of the smoking burned-out buildings ransacked by revolutionaries.

He turned, going on, and the farther he went, he saw that the hills got taller and the vegetation thicker. Now there were long-shadowed cactus-trees and tight, twisted, low-creeping thorny plants. Juan stopped to look for some cactus to suck on. But he was from the mountains, so he didn't know which plant to choose. He sat down to rest. His mouth felt so dry he was choking. But then he saw his mother in his mind's eye, searching for him with her eyes swollen with tears. He struggled to his feet to go on. But his feet hurt so much, he couldn't stand to touch the ground.

"Oh, Mamá," he cried, "please, help me!"

And he continued stumbling up the tracks, with his feet on fire.

Then, coming around a long uphill bend in the tracks, he saw something move ahead of him in the dim light of the going day. Quickly, he grabbed a rock. He figured it was a deer and so, if he got the chance, he'd hit it on the head and then break its neck so he could suck its blood and eat its meat.

But when he got closer to the rocks where he'd first seen movement, he saw nothing. He glanced all around; still, he saw nothing but long, dark shadows and the last little thin yellow veins of the evening light.

He was just beginning to believe that it had all been a mistake and he'd seen nothing, when suddenly, there, right before his very eyes—no more than twenty feet away between two small, low rocks—he saw the large round eyes of a jaguar, his spots visible in the dim light.

Juan froze.

"Oh, Mamá, Mamá," he said to himself, losing all courage as he stared at the big cat's eyes. And he wanted to turn and run, but the big cat's tail was now up and moving side to side like an upright snake, hypnotizing him.

The big cat shifted his feet, crouched down, getting ready to leap, and Juan knew this was his last chance to do something. But he was just too scared to move. Then, Juan heard his mother's voice inside him saying, "Attack him, *mi hijito!* Don't run! Attack! Or he'll kill you!"

"Yes, Mamá," he found himself saying. And he let out a howling roar with all his power and attacked the tiger of the desert.

The spotted tiger heard Juan's mighty roar and saw him coming at him in leaping bounds. The big animal leaped up, too, roaring out a terrible scream. But then he turned and ran.

Juan stopped dead in his tracks, turned tail, too, and took off up the side of the tracks as fast as his little legs could go. The big desert cat never looked back. He just kept racing in the other direction.

Juan's feet didn't hurt anymore, and he ran up the tracks without once slowing down until the sun was long gone and the moon came out.

He went all night—walking and running—until he came out of the other side of the small red-rock hills and the morning stars were his companions.

He ran, not stopping, not caring how much his bloody, swollen feet hurt or his throbbing head pained until, way up there in the distance in the darkish daybreak, he thought he saw the little flickering lights of a hundred campfires.

He slowed down, catching his breath, and he could hear people talking. He listened carefully as he came and then, up ahead in the middle of the flat, he saw the train—the train he'd been after all this time. He began to sob. He'd made it; he'd caught the train. He was going to be able to find his mother and family and not be lost forever and ever.

But then, getting near the campfires, he felt a strange anger come into him. So he circled around the camp—cautious as a coyote, wary as a young deer—making sure that they weren't bandits but were, indeed, his people.

One of the boys who'd raced with him saw him coming.

"Dios mío!" said the startled boy. "You came the whole way on foot, Juan?"

But Juan couldn't hear the boy, much less see him. Juan was gone. He was as white as a ghost. His whole face and neck and shoulders were white from where the salty sweat had dried on his skin. He was falling, stumbling, gasping, crying as he came toward their fires, white-lipped and wild-eyed.

"Your mother," said the boy, "she said you'd catch us. She told my father last night that you'd . . ."

But Juan paid no attention to the boy. He just walked on, staring at the fires ahead of him. He was hypnotized by the little leaping flames. He was dead on his feet. He'd been running half-conscious since he'd raced away in terror from the spotted desert tiger.

A man turned and saw Juan and leaped up, grabbing him under the armpits just before Juan pitched face-first into the fire.

But, still, Juan's feet kept climbing. He couldn't stop. He had to get past those little dancing hills of flaming fire so he could reach his mother, the love of his life, the only living thing that gave meaning to his entire existence.

*   *   *

Author's Note

I was driving back from Mexico City with my father when he told me this story for the umpteenth time. I was twenty years old, in great shape, could run a marathon with ease, and yet there was no way on earth that I could've pulled off this feat. But my father assured me over and over that it was absolutely true and he'd done this and he'd been nothing but a little boy.

"Listen, when you got fear pushing you," said my dad, "and love pulling you, you are capable of doing incredible things. You have to understand, I loved my mother more than life itself. I died several times that day, I'm sure, but I just kept living right through death itself. And that's what any human can do when he has that much love.

"Hate has given me power many times in my life, but not like love. Love is the greatest power we humans have. And also understand, *mi hijito*, that back then, we walked and ran everywhere we went. We, kids, didn't have horses. We had our feet, and they were as tough as nails. So, yes, it was a big feat, but not really so big when you realize how tough we all were back then and how much love I had for my mother."

My father and I drove all over that terrain north of León, Guanajuanto, and we came to realize that the distance he'd run must have been over a hundred miles and he'd done it without water or food. My God, I just knew to the bottom of my heart that he was right. No soldier or great athlete could have pulled off that feat. It took an ordinary boy with love in his heart to do the impossible. Because, after all, we, the ordinary people, are the real power here on earth when we have love in our hearts and magic in our souls.

Thank you, *gracias*.